To Bernard &

with love

and thanks

from Rosemary.

in remembrance of
the best holiday ever.

August 1980.

Street musicians ham it up in Zürich.

THIS BEAUTIFUL WORLD　VOL. 62

Switzerland

ELIZABETH POWERS
STEVE VIDLER

 KODANSHA INTERNATIONAL LTD.
TOKYO, NEW YORK & SAN FRANCISCO

Distributors:

UNITED STATES: *Kodansha International/USA, Ltd., through Harper & Row, Publishers, Inc., 10 East 53rd Street, New York, New York 10022.* SOUTH AMERICA: *Harper & Row, Publishers, Inc., International Department.* CANADA: *Fitzhenry & Whiteside Ltd., 150 Lesmill Road, Don Mills, Ontario M3B 2T6.* MEXICO AND CENTRAL AMERICA: *HARLA S. A. de C. V., Apartado 30–546, Mexico 4, D. F.* UNITED KINGDOM: *Phaidon Press Ltd., Littlegate House, St. Ebbe's Street, Oxford OX1 1SQ.* EUROPE: *Boxerbooks Inc., Limmatstrasse 111, 8031 Zürich.* AUSTRALIA AND NEW ZEALAND: *Book Wise (Australia) Pty. Ltd., 104–8 Sussex Street, Sydney 2000.* THE FAR EAST: *Toppan Company (S) Pte. Ltd., No. 38, Liu Fang Road, Jurong, Singapore 22.*

Published by Kodansha International Ltd., 2-12-21 Otowa, Bunkyo-ku, Tokyo 112 and Kodansha International/USA, Ltd., 10 East 53rd Street, New York, New York 10022 and 44 Montgomery Street, San Francisco, California 94104. Copyright in Japan 1978 by Kodansha International Ltd. All rights reserved. Printed in Japan.

LCC 77–15297
ISBN 0–87011–327–5
JBC 0326–786201–2361

First edition, 1978

Contents

Introduction 7
Four Cities 31
Excursions 83
The Playground of Europe 101
Tips for Travelers 135

It is a small country, 15,941 square miles to be exact, about half the size of the state of Maine. It has a population of approximately six and a half million. There are twenty-five largely autonomous states, or cantons as the Swiss call them. And it is located smack in the center of Western Europe: the Federal Republic of Germany to the north, Austria to the east, Italy to the south, and France to the west. On this patch of rocky soil—this point of convergence of three European cultures—the Swiss nation developed. Today, it comprises four linguistic groups and is a country that defies the premise that religious, linguistic, or ethnic unity makes a nation. There are German Swiss (sixty-five per cent), French Swiss (eighteen per cent), and Italian Swiss (twelve per cent). There is even a small relic group, the Romansh-speaking Swiss (.08 per cent), restricted to the eastern canton of Grisons. All have their individual customs, languages, house and settlement patterns. The portions of the country they inhabit bear the imprint of their different heritages. The designations themselves (e.g., German Swiss) do not refer to any political entity, however. The Swiss, of whatever heritage, have probably the strongest national identity of any people in Europe today.

What created this unity from diversity? What brought them all together? Why didn't they join up with their similar-tongued brethren? From the eleventh century the area that is now Switzerland was, like most of Europe, part of the Holy Roman Empire; but in the absence of any coherent rule, it became a thoroughly feudal society, with the peasants inevitably oppressed by taxes and tithes, and the nobility running their domains pretty much according to their own fancy. By the twelfth century there were a few towns—Zürich, Bern, Basel, for instance—in which some kind of civic spirit reigned, the result of a phenomenon on the rise all over Europe: expanding trade and a growing merchant class.

Whether Wilhelm Tell ever lived is uncertain, but the events surrounding his legend bring to life one of the outstanding Swiss traits, the desire for freedom, for independence from authority. Three communities on Lake Luzern—the forest cantons of Uri, Schwyz (from which the name "Switzerland" derives), and Unterwalden—had for a long time enjoyed a measure of immunity from their overlords and had learned to cooperate to avoid starvation. Perhaps much like the Bostonians many centuries later, they eventually resolved to take matters more into their own hands, and in 1291 they formed a perpetual alliance, swearing an oath at Rütli to settle disagreements by arbitration and to come to each other's aid when attacked. One of the West's first freedom movements was born.

These actions did not sit well with their Hapsburg rulers, but the latter had other irons in the fire all over the Empire, and the three cantons enjoyed their autonomy for a while. Luzern, a neighbor on the lake, joined the Everlasting League in 1332, and then Zürich in 1351. These cities and rural districts strengthened their political independence through numerous armed conflicts, and by 1388 the Swiss Confederation (now including Bern, Glarus, and Zug as well) had become a reality, and the confederates had learned the lessons of cooperation. They had won their independence. The confederation survived the vicissitudes of the following centuries, and in 1815 it bade welcome to Geneva—the last canton to join. Except for some minor modifications, the borders of Switzerland have remained fixed since 1815, and in the same year permanent Swiss neutrality was recognized by the Western powers; it was reaffirmed in the 1920 Declaration of London and, in the years of the Nazi menace, it left Switzerland marooned, but uninvaded.

Never during these centuries could the alliance be described as a comfortable one. What was it that held the land together, sealed truly in perpetuity, when so many nations around the world have treated us to the spectacle of minor differences exploding into civil warfare? Geography has a lot to do with it. There are no great open spaces in Switzerland. One-quarter of the land is uncultivable high Alps, lakes, and rock. The abundant natural resources that Switzerland's neighbors possess are absent here, and a high percentage of its raw materials, fuel, and food is imported via costly land routes. What it possesses are the will and industry of its inhabitants, a population intent on protecting its hard-won freedom. Endowed by nature with the basis for no more than a meager pastoral economy, the Swiss have managed to achieve one of the highest standards of living in the world, and Swiss products have become synonymous with high quality.

The Swiss may not be wild about their neighbors in the next canton; they may even be suspicious of the denizens of the next village because of some prejudice nurtured for generations. What is notably absent is that divisiveness that taints my own melting-pot homeland. Despite very strong cantonal autonomy ("states' rights," one might say), a proper balance of competing interests is usually achieved when concrete problems face the entire country—the problem of national security, for example. The Swiss have seen the wisdom of "united we stand, divided we fall." Theirs is not an idle nation. From necessity, they are rather more realistic, cautious, and prudent than some other peoples when it comes to innovations or in the use of what they have. They are thrifty and disciplined—notably Germanic traits, but their discipline has been tempered by French and Italian influences.

The convergence on one soil of different cultures, together with the topography of Switzerland which itself would have been sufficient to make parochialism a national trait, have prevented the development of a distinctive "Swiss" culture. Switzerland has, however, had an ample share of eminent men of letters and science. Le Corbusier is only the most famous exponent of Swiss architectural expertise. One cannot discuss modern psychology without speaking of C. G. Jung. Major artists include Alberto Giacometti and (though German-born, later a Swiss citizen) Paul Klee. World-famous writers range from Jean-Jacques Rousseau to Hermann Hesse and Max Frisch. Add film director Alain Tanner, composer Arthur Honegger, and theologian Karl Barth. Zürich's Federal Institute of Technology has produced more Nobel Prize recipients than any other science school in the world. In addition, Switzerland's role as a haven from war and its laws of political asylum have drawn creative minds throughout the years—among them, James Joyce, Lenin, and Thomas Mann, all of whom spent a good deal of time in Switzerland. Cultural entertainment in Switzerland also testifies to a people interested in more than just precision watches. Zürich enjoys a great wealth of museums and cultural life. Lugano (pop. 30,000) is the home of the Villa Favorita, probably the finest private art collection in Europe. Bern's Art Museum houses the world's largest collection of paintings and drawings by Paul Klee. And during the week that I was in St. Gallen (pop. 80,000), five different plays and one opera were presented at the City Theater.

Internationally, the Swiss have maintained their beloved neutrality. Far from retreating into alpine fastnesses, however, they offer the world the benefits of their special position through humanitarian activities (the 150th birthday anniversary of the founder of the Red Cross, Jean-Henri Dunant, was celebrated in 1978) and through their "good offices": Switzerland, for instance, is diplomatic middleman for about fifty countries that aren't on speaking terms.

Can we speak of an "average" Swiss? Let me try to describe a few. One is from a village near Appenzell, in east Switzerland, and he is a dairy farmer. The herd is small, but his is the typical unit of production in what eventually contributes to one-half of all Switzerland's agricultural income. With his strong build, blond hair, and ruddy face, he might be a character in *Tannhäuser*. A master cheese-maker for his village, he rises at 4:30 every morning to await the arrival of milk from the other villagers. His day is long and hard, for he still performs by hand all the stages in the time-consuming process of making cheese.

If our average Swiss is a banker from Zürich, he won't have "Tannhäuser's" brawn, for he is mostly indoors, in one of those solid nineteenth-century structures on the Bahnhofstrasse (which despite their age do nothing to suggest that anything is wrong with the financial system of Switzerland). His dress is a little on the conservative side, but his glasses and hairstyle show an awareness of changing trends; and unless promoted to the "inner sanctum" of his firm, he will use public transportation when he goes out to conduct business. He is always on the move, but still finds time now and again to spend a few minutes in one of the numerous cafés on the streets of Zürich.

Or he may be the bright-eyed young man from Luzern, with longish hair and frameless glasses, who still wears the "native" shirts he bought on a recent six-month trip to India and Nepal. He studies languages. His future plans? To work for the Red Cross.

He may be a vintner from Epesses, a wine village above Lake Geneva (Lac Léman), a big, sturdy, somewhat rowdy type, about whom one might have second thoughts before starting a fight. His solidity derives in part from the back-breaking hours he puts in on his sloping vineyards. Still, as he sits over his decanter of wine after a hard day's work, he unbends, laughs roughly, cracks jokes with his French-speaking companions, and mocks the frailty of his "God-damned" vines.

If he lives in Lausanne, just down the road from Epesses, he might be a lawyer. Switzerland has probably produced as many distinguished lawyers and jurists as bankers, due to the need to establish a legal code that would be fair in a "mosaic," a population of very varied background. He may look as earnest as that banker in Zürich, but the aura of competence is relieved by a certain lightness and calm.

If he comes from Lugano, he may be a clerk, doctor, lawyer, or businessman, but his behavior will be a fusion of Italian grace and what is called native efficiency. To see him sitting over his two-hour lunch—with his flashing brown eyes, his gentleness, his bombast—you would think you were in Rome or Milan; but, like the next man, he will put in eight hard hours at his office.

He may be a farmer from Grisons and be part of the small Romansh group, who in feature—and rarity—reminded me of the Gaeltacht inhabitants of Ireland, the native Irish speakers. Of a traditional beauty—rather fine-boned, with swimming blue eyes, rosy pink cheeks, and dark curly hair—he is a member of a quiet, proud lot.

Or he may be one of the new Swiss. Fifteen years ago he came from Spain (by now the flow of foreign workers is drying up), worked hard, liked Switzerland, sent for his wife, spent the requisite number of years in the country, and became a Swiss citizen. He is now manager of an alpine resort restaurant in the Bernese Oberland. As he promenades around town on Sunday afternoon with his family, playfully carrying his daughter on his shoulders, with a certain erectness and pride and, yes, *Bürgerlichkeit* about him, he is indistinguishable from many of his fellow citizens.

These "miniatures," perhaps, seem merely an expansion of my original list of images. More stereotypes, you may say. If so, I have done Switzerland an injustice. This is a country without homogeneity, a people imbued with the manners of the region—the village, in many cases—from which they come. Unlike the gnome, though—that ageless, deformed creature who lives underground, intent only on guarding his treasure—the Swiss, while maintaining their own customs, have learned to like and assimilate diversity, and are well liked in return.

Vive la Suisse! Viva la Svizzera! Hoch lebe die Schweiz!

1. Zürich's Grossmünster Cathedral (*preceding page*) was Charlemagne's ninth-century memorial to the missionaries who converted the city to Christianity. The statue is of Hans Waldmann, a wealthy medieval adventurer and political strongman.

2–3. Streetcars (*below*) and newsstands crammed with domestic and foreign magazines are a common sight on the streets of Switzerland's largest city.

4. Automatic ticket vendors have helped streamline city travel.

5. Elsewhere, in Zürich's less harassed streets, the Swiss have been visibly reluctant to modernize.

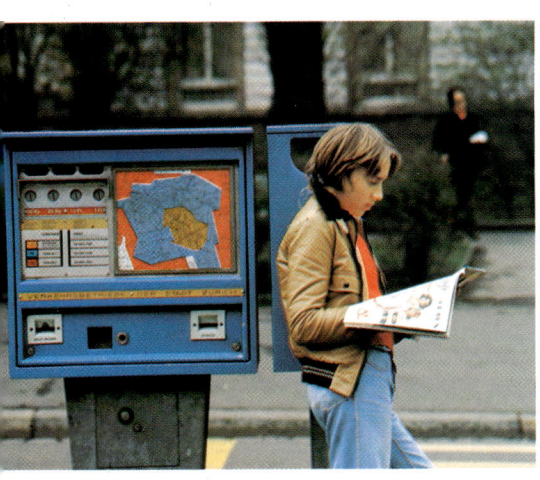

6. A grandmother, with her grandchild and a large new doll, in town to visit relatives.

7. Pretty participants (*right*) in Zürich's "Sechsläuten" festival, held in April.

8. The girl *below* runs a stall at the weekend flea market in Zürich.

9. Placed on "pedestals," policewomen direct traffic in Zürich's busier thoroughfares.

10. An afternoon sun casts long shadows across a game of chess in one of Zürich's public squares. The spires of St. Peter's and the Fraumünster rise beyond.

11. About half of the Swiss work force is involved in the manufacture of commercial goods. The confectionery industry alone (*left*) comprises over seven hundred concerns that employ some fifty thousand people.

12. One humble product of the chocolate industry finds a customer's small, sticky hand (*below*).

13. 1191 is the date traditionally ascribed to the founding of Bern, and in 1353 it became the eighth canton to join the Swiss Confederation. The heraldic devices of twenty-two cantons can be seen in Bern's Parliament Building.

14. *Below* is the "House" of the Parliament Building.

15. The Zytgloggeturm, or clock tower, *left*, has been furnishing Bern with chiming entertainment since 1530.

16. The Old City of Bern, *below*, is compressed within a narrow loop of the Aare River.

17. Perhaps the most popular Bern landmark is the Bear Pit, where bears have been kept since 1513. One legend has it that Bern's founder, the Duke of Zähringen, named his new outpost after the first animal he killed on a hunt.

18. A Bernese delicatessen, with heaped sandwiches called *Belegte Brote* in the foreground.

19. On the shores of Lake Geneva, Lausanne is dominated by the early Gothic cathedral of Notre Dame, consecrated in 1275.

20. Conspicuous *below* are Lausanne's Old Academy and the square bulk of the Château St. Maire, formerly the bishop's palace.

21. Inn signs decorate a corner of the Old City of Lausanne; the spire of the cathedral eavesdrops behind.

22. Lugano, *overleaf*, is a sunny resort in ▷ the southern canton of Ticino, built on the edge of a narrow, twisting lake.

23–25. Strongly reminiscent of neighboring Italy in climate and character, Lugano is best explored on foot—along the crooked alleys of its lakeside quarter. The Ticinese cuisine is best explored on an empty stomach—with plenty of local wine.

26. Steamers, *overleaf*, provide leisurely excursions to a string of pretty villages, perched on the shores of Lake Lugano.

are Swiss who have been drawn to the cities for work, and there are others who were born and raised among the sounds of streetcars and the sight of streetlights. But because they are always within half an hour of mountains, pastures, lakes, or rivers, both are very conscious of nature and eager to emulate its effects in their urban environment.

From the moment I saw Zürich, for example, I knew Swiss cities would not be those urban nightmares one encounters elsewhere in the world. Due to a fortunate abundance of water, industry is mostly driven electrically; indeed, one can pass through industrialized parts of Zürich and barely register the presence of machinery. Likewise, most public transport runs on electric power, so there's less noxious exhaust to blur the view or congest the lungs. Where many other cities have squalid urban patches, Swiss ones have flowers and litterless streets. "Painfully clean," said my Swiss friend Ursula about Regensberg, a village outside Zürich where the flowers surrounding the wooden houses knocked my eyes out, with nary a scrap of paper or a cigarette butt to offend the scene. And, happily, this cleanliness and delight in decoration are carried over to the cities.

Market day is also an occasion that affirms the ties between city and country. This twice-weekly event transforms paved public squares into orchards and gardens, and is experienced with great enthusiasm by city-dweller and country folk alike. There are stalls with cheeses rank and mild, stalls with bananas and apples, flowers, and meat. The prices are no cheaper than in the stores, but who does not feel that life is somehow richer and fuller when he can browse and choose among hundreds of stalls overflowing with the bounty of the land? I often had the feeling that the Swiss put away their cares on market days, and that playful, aesthetic considerations governed their choices. How beautiful a shopping basket full of daisies, fat red radishes, shiny green and yellow peppers, and a fragrant loaf of fresh brown bread!

Swiss cities are not as large as their counterparts elsewhere in Europe. Zürich is the largest, with a population of 450,000. For the tourist, everything of interest is within walking distance, certainly within the reach of trolley, streetcar, or bus. One isn't overwhelmed physically by a day in town. In Zürich, an actress told me that she and her husband had moved out to the countryside because they found life in the city too hectic. After experiencing the rigors of Tokyo for several years, it took me several trips back to Zürich after visiting other parts of Switzerland to have the faintest idea of what she found hectic there.

On the plane to Switzerland, my neighbor said that Zürich was the only interesting city in Switzerland. People in Lausanne swear by the superiority of their city and life-style over Zürich—over all east Switzerland in fact. A woman in Fribourg declared that she wouldn't live in Lausanne under any circumstances. I began to feel that these prejudices reflected the tenacity of local customs. And confirmation appeared in the form of a nineteenth-century writer's wonderful description of one Swiss village: "The villagers here are very constant and cling to their old customs. If a stone falls from a wall, the same stone will be put back; new houses are built in the style of old ones; damaged roofs are repaired with the same kind of tiles; and if one household raises checked cows, it will always raise checked cows and the house will be known by the pattern."

ZÜRICH

Let me start where most travelers begin their trips to Switzerland, in Zürich. One gets off the plane at Kloten Airport, heads for the front of the terminal, and catches a city-bound bus, as I did, on a cool, sunny day in May. My fellow passengers were mostly well-dressed, middle-aged burghers, many with dogs. I would encounter these people and an astonishing variety of dogs ("It's a dog's life" takes on a different significance here) everywhere in Switzerland.

In every city I visited the first thing I undertook was a city tour by bus. Tourist groups are much the same throughout the world (American women always seem to have flimsy shoes, while their German counterparts wear rigid-looking things; the French are incredibly insulted if you address them in English, and there is always someone obsessed with locating a toilet as your group files into some medieval cathedral). There are also annoyances and confusions in being chanted to in three languages (earphones would be helpful; the guide invariably repeats the German explanation twice and forgets the French one, much to the exasperation of the Gallic element). All in all, though, the tours proceed in comfort and with the minimum of fuss. These quick trips are ideal for introducing the key attractions, and the result is often a desire to return and savor on one's own.

Zürich is a beautifully situated city, lying at the head of a long ribbon of water, from which flows the Limmat River, whose current glides through the city's old quarter. This quarter, the Altstadt, is the heart of Zürich, and it was on the left bank of the Limmat that the Romans established a military outpost in the second century. Zürich's fast-growing cultural and political importance is shown by the fact that the foundations of two great cathedrals, the Grossmünster and Fraumünster, were already laid in the ninth century on the right bank. In 1218, Zürich became a free Imperial City, and by this time a settlement of merchants and artisans had appeared around the cathedrals. Zürich's nobles never quite had the upper hand here, and the artisans—the real political force—quickly recognized that their best interests lay in joining the other Swiss confederates, which they did in 1351. The city's acceptance of Huguenots and other religious dissidents in the sixteenth century stimulated the pulse—already strong—of commerce and trade, and the first industry, silk, was launched. The rest is history, as they say. Unlike other European cities that went out of business after a time of prominence, Zürich has continued to grow in stature and importance and is now one of the most prosperous industrial cities in all Europe.

An early Saturday morning walk from my hotel brought me right into this historical heartland. At the Fraumünster, on one of the benches that are scattered about the large open square, I would sit with a coffee and pastry I had bought at one of the stands that are set up for market day. Swans swam in the clear water of the Limmat, and steamers stood in sparkling readiness for those intent on outings on the lake. The crowds were not about yet, but the fruit, vegetable, and flower merchants were arranging wares on their stalls, hundreds of them, along the Limmatquai, and behind them rose the two Gothic towers of the Romanesque Grossmünster.

I found the Fraumünster side more picturesque, but proceeding from either of these cathedrals one can spend hours exploring the narrow streets of the old quarter. Preserved are excellent guild houses and bourgeois homes from past centuries, memorials to the sweat and power of these good citizens. I have never been one to care for specifics—whether that splendid rococo house at No. 20 Münsterhof (in front of the Fraumünster) housed the wine guild, or whether that was the very window the distinguished writer looked out of while composing his masterpiece (James Joyce wrote a large part of *Ulysses* during his years in Zürich). More interesting is the way people interact with these monuments of their past. Do they tear them down (New York), do they preserve them like museum pieces (Rome), or do they make them part of their lives?

In Zürich, it is the last, due in part to the Swiss tendency to maintain, to use what they have instead of throwing it away. The old quarter has, indeed, very few new structures. These old buildings are lived in, but many have been converted into stores and restaurants. Stores selling gems and gold jewelry, leather goods, the latest Paris fashions. Stunning displays of breads and cheeses, all the croissants and Gruyères and Emmentalers invitingly arranged in the windows. Art galleries, old books, and etchings to tempt the browser. Elegant, intimate restaurants at every corner. Stained-glass windows, and frescoes that dominate entire facades.

Moving on from here, away from the lake, one comes to the Bahnhofstrasse. Down this wide street, lined with slender trees, smart shops, and sidewalk cafés glide Zürich's extraterrestrial streetcars. Whenever I was in the Bahnhofstrasse, Zürich's other major shopping and amusement area, I enjoyed popping into the basement of the big Globus department store and buying a piece of cheesecake and milk, grabbing a newspaper, and heading out to Pestalozzi Square in front of Globus. This little patch of green is hardly a match for the parks in other Swiss cities, but half the people who walk by succumb to the temptation to "take the weight off their feet" on one of the benches around the square, while genuine idlers like myself are willingly seduced by the sun and stretch out on the grass.

It is said that the German Swiss have only love of toil and do not know how to enjoy themselves. Efficiency and order don't occur naturally, it's true; they have to be worked at. Yet I could never get over my impression of Zürich as an overgrown village, a prosperous, lively one, no doubt, but a village just the same.

If one takes a streetcar from the central part of town to the adjoining suburbs of Enge or Wollishofen, the large, elegant houses there provide ample testimony to the earthly rewards of hard work; yet the splash of geraniums or begonias in the windows is always enough to dispel any feeling one might have that bad humor has to be a by-product of labor.

Strengthening this village impression was a festival I happened to see one day in Zürich. I was going down to the Limmatquai one Saturday afternoon in June to see a movie. On the streetcar was a prosperous-looking couple with two children, the kind one is more likely to see riding around in a Mercedes than on public transport. They hurriedly disembarked at the Limmatquai, rushed over to one of the cafés where some friends had saved places for them, and sat down. Since there was a great crowd about, I also waited; not ten minutes later a parade of music and folk-dance groups began, everyone in traditional dress, from villages and towns all over Switzerland. When each regional group swung into view a great shout went up from scattered partisans in the crowd—neighbors, probably, from the same town—and this rooting and clapping continued the entire two hours of the procession. But Zürich's biggest romp, held every April, is the "Sechsläuten" festival—an occasion which, some would say, allows citizens to express emotions that have been held in check all year by a strong work ethic. And for two days there is wild merrymaking, the costumes and masks of the participants keeping Canons and Kodaks busy.

The people of Zürich, in common with all the Swiss, share a love for good eating and drinking establishments, and as in other big cities there is something special about evening in such places. The daily grind is over and "the night is young." The action switches to the Niederdorf, which runs toward the Grossmünster. This is an area alive with cafés, pizza parlors, sausage bars (unbeatable prices), movies, restaurants, and go-go bars; and it is definitely *the* place to imbibe Zürich's after-hours atmosphere.

Walking slowly along the Niederdorf one evening I saw a group of people huddled together in a somber cluster in front of a café, a guitar player strumming a frail tune while another member handed out brochures about "inner satisfaction and happiness" to customers inside. I couldn't, for the life of me, see how their dismal singing could possibly raise men's spirits. But I needn't have worried: no preacher's tract was going to distract a Zürcher intent on enjoying his evening out.

LAUSANNE

Swiss hotels and hostelry are probably the most reliable in the world. In fact, with their reputation for service and cleanliness, one would be hard put to find a bad hotel anywhere in Switzerland. In Lausanne, though, after some searching, I managed to find one, the eternal exception. It was not really an extensive search. Switzerland is a convention country, and I think doctors or dentists were occupying all the two-, three-, four-, and five-star hotels when I was there. Since I was lucky to get one at all, I'll gloss over all the details—the Italian maids staring mournfully whenever I passed through the hall, the same fingerprints on the mirror day after day—for it was a place to lay one's head for a few days.

Above all, I was deprived there of an experience that remains among my favorite in Switzerland: breakfast in bed. I soon discovered that if one wanted to feel like more than an ordinary mortal first thing in the morning one had merely to pick up the phone. What luxury! Steaming pots of coffee and milk, bread and rolls, butter, jam, and cheese would result—a gentle and indulgent entry into the world. Afterward one could emerge and face whatever adventures might await one with equanimity, ask for directions in broken French, wander for hours uphill and downhill (Lausanne is very hilly) with cameras slung from one's long-suffering shoulders, and experiment with unfamiliar menus.

The first meal I had in Lausanne was in a small bistro. The food was *saucisse aux choux*, homemade sausage with cabbage, which was a specialty of the region and well worth trying. But it was the Gallic flavor of the place, with five or six longish tables that could seat eight snugly (and one dog underneath), the men sipping their coffee and reading *Le Figaro*, the three motherly waitresses who served carafes of wine, salads, baskets of bread, and insisted that the customers finish every bite on their plates, the warmth, the graciousness, the intimacy—it was these that I loved.

Food and drink and the surroundings in which they are enjoyed occupy an important place in this part of Switzerland. My parents happened to be in Europe on a tour when we met up in Lausanne, and together we ventured to the Chalet Suisse, high above Lausanne, for *fondue*. Traditional *fondue* is a mixture of white wine and strong cheese, with a bit of kirsch and garlic, which is kept gently bubbling in a casserole by a small methylated spirit lamp underneath. If the mixture grows cold it separates and congeals into a sticky mass of cheese and alcohol. Eating *fondue* off a plate would be disastrous. What you do is tear off pieces of bread and keep them on your plate, ready to be speared with special long forks and dipped into the *fondue*. You then wash down the rich dish with great mouthfuls of wine. My father, a confirmed beer drinker, insisting that the Swiss Chalet in Louisville, Kentucky, had let him drink beer with his *fondue*, suffered the contempt of one conservative waiter, for whom the suggestion was nothing short of barbarous.

Only a beer drinker could resist the charms of the fragrant, light, white wines of this region—among them, Chablais, Dézaley, and Saint-Saphorin. One of my first views, as the train edged toward Lausanne, was of the southward-sloping vineyards basking in the sun that reflects off Lake Geneva. Hills and mountains in the background protect the grapes from the chilling effect of north winds, and this vast curving shore, terraced like an amphitheater, is the largest unbroken stretch of vineyards in Switzerland. It is just a short ride from Lausanne to the wine-producing villages, whose cool stone houses and quiet streets are themselves like wine cellars.

The Lausanne City Tour included a visit to one of these villages, and the seven on our tour did a worthy job of polishing off the several bottles of wine we were treated to. Though we were a small group, we were probably fairly representative of the motley crews that make up such sightseeing tours: two honeymooning Italians who couldn't speak French, English, German, or Spanish (the guide's languages), but were too preoccupied to care; two Greeks who spoke French and a smattering of Italian, and who tried their best to translate the guide's comments for the Italians; and two other Americans besides myself, one an adventurous, elderly lady whom I was later to encounter often, making her way about Lausanne. (Although she was staying in the deluxe Beau Rivage Hotel at $100 a day, she was quite thrilled when I explained to her how to get about Lausanne on the mini-subway.) We had all entered the bus with our stock of prejudices and the greatest mistrust of one another, but in the end we were toasting each other's health and wealth and happiness. Such is the potency of the wine of this area.

Lausanne begins at Ouchy, on Lake Geneva (the Lausannois seem to resent one calling it this; for them it is Lac Léman). The atmospheric conditions that contribute to the grape's vitality—the southern exposure, shelter from the north, reflected solar radiation, balanced temperature—produce brilliant scenery and imbue the place with what can only be called a luminous character. With the breathtaking background of the glittering Alps and the majestic outlines of the Dents du Midi and Mont Blanc on the south side of the lake, the Riviera-style luxury hotels, the tree- and flower-lined promenade, the inviting lakeshore restaurants and cafés, hundreds of yachts moored in the harbor, smart pleasure steamers stopping in, Ouchy is superb.

Despite the fact that Lausanne was "Reformed" and that the austerity of Calvin's Geneva was felt in the city, a particularly brilliant intellectual life has reigned here and in neighboring towns along the lake for centuries. Voltaire and Edward Gibbon were enthusiastic admirers of Lausanne. Madame de Staël's château in Coppet, just a short ride by boat from Lausanne, was a lively literary center in the nineteenth century. To the other side of Lausanne on the lake, past the resort of Montreux, is the castle of Chillon, which Lord Byron visited with the poet Shelley. Byron's poem "The Prisoner of Chillon" is about the freethinking François Bonivard, an inhabitant who was probably oblivious to the beautiful setting. See if the dungeon at the castle, where Bonivard spent six gloomy years chained to a post, doesn't still chill your blood, after all the passing centuries.

The lakeside is not all of Lausanne, however. The city stretches up over three hills, to be crowned by the Cathedral of Notre Dame, Switzerland's most important early Gothic cathedral. Lausanne is the capital of the French-speaking canton of Vaud, the home of the Swiss Supreme Court, and an important commercial center. Up in Cité (reached quite easily by Lausanne's mini-subway, the top station of an otherwise heart-thumping climb), one is near the traffic maelstrom of the Place St. François and the most prominent monuments of Lausanne. Besides the cathedral, there is the fifteenth-century town hall, the beautiful, baroque Ancien Hôpital, and the fifteenth-century castle of St. Maire. Particularly recommended are long walks along the tilting cobblestone streets of this quarter, where one can always encounter Lausanne's saltier types pouring down a glass of wine or whiskey.

On Wednesdays and Saturdays the Place de la Riponne fills with farmers and merchants. Just as the Swiss value quality when producing goods, so they are also demanding and eclectic buyers. The displays of cheese and bread, fruits, and vegetables compare favorably with those in the city's shops. For me Lausanne's market also featured some memorable "finds." One was the most extensive collection of old European postcards I have ever laid eyes on, album upon album of hand-tinted portly beauties of 1890, marching soldiers of 1914, steamers plying the Swiss lakes in the summer season, greetings in verse for all occasions. A few cheap-souvenir salesmen were also doing brisk business. One little device being hawked with humor and lengthy extemporaneous exposition was a battery-powered alarm, to be worn on one's person, which let out an ear-splitting sound when its owner felt threatened, or just unwanted. It struck me that the salesmen could be doing better business in New York than on these clear shores.

BERN

"Wow! This place has everything," I heard a backpacker exclaim after arriving by train in Bern. The object of his admiration was not the city but the station building itself, which housed showers and bathrooms, lockers, telephone and teletype facilities, beauty and barber shops, cafés, restaurants, stand-up bars, banks, newspaper and magazine stands, grocery stores, and God knows what else. One could conduct one's entire social and business life here.

Standing on the border of Old Bern and New Bern, this modern station does in fact play an important part in the vitality of this "jewel of a medieval town," as Bern is often called; and though Bern has its rivals among other Swiss and European cities, few can match its urban vitality.

It has been said of Bern that its picturesqueness is reminiscent of Germany, its houses of France, and its arcades of Italy. Whatever the case, the characteristic architecture of Bern—the pleasing unity of the house style, the four miles of arcades, the wide cobblestone streets—was planned by its founder, Duke Berchtold V of Zähringen in 1191, although most of today's buildings date from the eighteenth century (fires had a way with medieval towns). The Old City is located within the protected bend of the Aare River, and its homogeneous architecture presents a fascinating picture when viewed early in the morning from the Rose Garden, at the southern end of the present-day city. Gerechtigkeitsgasse, Junkerngasse, Münstergasse—all those grand-sounding streets are full of solid patrician houses with red-tiled roofs. There are a dozen colorful fountains dating from the sixteenth century. A clock tower from 1530 rings in each hour with marching bears and jesters, an armored horseman, and a crowing cock. Indeed, I wouldn't be surprised if Bern were officially certified as picturesque, for it has all the charming historical features that non-European tourists appreciate on their trips to the Continent. But Bern is not a museum piece; in all those broad cobblestone streets and arcades the life of the capital of Switzerland is actively lived out.

To preserve the Old City's historic character, the renovation and rebuilding of structures within its walls must be approved by the local government and must harmonize with existing buildings. Considerable time and money are also spent on the interiors, as I got a chance to see one day. It was a house in Junkerngasse, where I had peeped in at an exhibit of paintings by the Spanish artist Pepe España. The house was a four-story affair, with two rooms on either side of the landing as one went up, and the paintings were hung on the walls of the staircase and in the rooms of the top floor. A skylight at the top of the stairwell flooded light down onto the paintings and the gleam of polished wooden floors in a discreetly modern setting. The major problem of keeping these fine houses in good shape is money, and it would be a shame if only the very rich could afford to live in them.

The fountains of Bern face no such problem. Their preservation has been amply provided for by the generosity of a master shoemaker of Bern, a certain Mr. Loesch, whose civic pride prompted him to leave his fortune to the City of Bern solely for the upkeep of the fountains. The fountains once served as a meeting place for the people, who had to fetch all their water for cooking, washing, and drinking from them, and one must admire the instincts of the long-dead Bernese who made sure they remained attractive.

As in all Swiss cities, if you can use your legs you can see Bern easily (and the City Tour here gets a five-star rating from me). The local tourist office provides a free map of the city, obtainable at the railway station. The Old City is shown in relief, and a suggested walking tour is drawn in with a blue dotted line; the points of interest are numbered and explained in four languages.

By following this map one proceeds in one full day through the arcades, probably Bern's most characteristic feature. Built in front of the houses and projecting over the huge sidewalks, for almost eight hundred years these arcades have been a covered way for pedestrians, merchants, and craftsmen. It is no different today. Even the cellars, into which one descends from the streets, serve as cubbyholes for wine bars, dress shops, some good restaurants, and even a Sex Supermarket.

The walking tour also allows for a lingering look at the fountains, of which my favorite was the one representing Justice. The sculptures on the main portal of the cathedral deserve close inspection, too. The Last Judgment, with its 283 figures making their final journey to heaven or hell, all packed together and looking terrified of missing their connection (much like the Japanese on their commuter trains), remains a powerful sculpture, even in these godless times. The same also applies to the life-size apostles, prophets, and Wise and Foolish Virgins that have been recently restored on the main portal.

Then there is the Bear Pit of Bern. For some reason, bears and Bern are closely associated, and a bear is displayed on Bern's flag. Many explanations have been given, some etymological, some concerning the presence of bears in the area in the Middle Ages. The real historical reason we may never know, but I did learn some interesting things about these animals, of which more than twenty make their home in the deep pit near Nydegg Bridge. A full-grown bear, for instance, may weigh up to five hundred and fifty pounds, but at birth it is probably a meager ten to twelve ounces. In captivity bears easily live thirty years without showing their age. A she-bear gives birth to her first young, usually one or two, at three to five years; the cubs are blind for about a month, and after approximately eight to nine weeks they begin walking. And they all looked quite happy and chubby, especially Mary and Susy, the babies—bombarbed as they are with carrots and dried fruit.

Bern has some excellent museums, for those inevitable rainy days. The Historical Museum contains much of what was plundered in medieval wars by the powerful Bernese nobility. Among other things, the Art Museum has a great number of Paul Klee's paintings and drawings. But my personal favorite among Bernese museums was the Swiss Postal Museum with its displays of stamps and a most fascinating group of exhibits on the development of posts and communications in Switzerland—communications being vital in this obviously land-locked country. There are maps of early postal routes (twice-weekly connections already between Zürich and Geneva in 1677); a copy of an 1881 Basel telephone book (who were the privileged owners of a copy of this 4" × 6", eight-page booklet?); an 1845 St. Gallen–Heiden horse-drawn postal coach painted in the same colors as today's buses; switchboards from 1885; and a railway carriage showing how mail is sorted en route.

Bern is an extremely friendly city, a place where strangers feel welcome. In restaurants, the proprietor can be seen making the rounds of customers' tables, spending a few minutes at each. And guests aren't pressured to leave within five minutes of closing time, the result being an atmosphere much like a private party, the clientele lingering over their food, off-duty waiters sitting around playing cards. Señor España, the painter, is just one of many expatriates drawn to Bern by the lure of such congenial facilities. Another that I met was a transplanted Portuguese, Thea Fuchs, who is married to a Bernese and operates a restaurant there by the name of the Swiss Chalet. One of the relatively few places in Switzerland where traditional Swiss entertainment is offered, it attracts visitors who are fond of linking arms and swinging back and forth to rousing music after several bottles of wine. Mrs. Fuchs, fluent in six languages, makes them feel—not "at home," no, better than that, alive and having fun. And even I overcame my innate misgivings about yodeling, for elegant Therese Wirthe von Kännel proved to be an excellent exponent of this endemic art.

LUGANO

I arrived in Lugano, in Italian-speaking Switzerland, from Italy. In this fashion it was interesting to speculate on what was "Swiss" and what was "Italian" about this part of Switzerland. I would swear it was when we crossed the border, but at a certain point in the bus ride the landscape starts putting itself into some kind of order. The houses are just as colorful and the flowers just as lush and abundant in Lugano as they are on the other side of the border, but a sense of method, of neatness asserts itself. The roads are wider and free of litter, the drivers more considerate, the roses have been pruned, and the color wash on the houses has not faded. The Italian Swiss are like the Swiss everywhere, gardeners in their own garden. On the other hand, many of those specific traits that people find endearing in Italians are evident in this part of Switzerland: wild gesticulation while speaking, bombast, intense solemnity at one's job, a love of children. The climate, of course, which is somewhat Mediterranean, mild and southern, except during the winter months, plays a role; for Italians would not be Italian if they suffered under cold temperatures nine months a year. And the same could be said about the Italian-speaking Swiss if they had settled around Basel a few hundred years ago.

Lugano itself is an imposing, pretty city. Deposited by bus right on the lakeshore, surrounded by palms and bougainvillea, my first impression was of another Riviera. In Switzerland, resorts are as common and varied as mountains and lakes. Lugano, for instance, is not the type of resort where dinner-table talk revolves around the conditions of the snow on the ski slopes that day (although Ticino is an alpine region and mountain sports are not out of the question). The major resorts in the canton of Ticino—Lugano, Ascona, and Locarno—belong in the same category as Acapulco and Miami Beach and St. Tropez, in the sense that visitors go there to participate in sports (but not to the point of exhaustion), get a suntan, relax, and enjoy themselves—to try on new personalities or shed old ones, and socialize. Splendid hotels, restaurants, sports facilities, cultural offerings, entertainment, even gambling, and elegant shops in which to purchase the necessary clothing for public life are abundant here. In addition, Lugano is a well-appointed base for exploring the lake.

The proportions and solidity of the buildings in the central part of Lugano around the Piazza Riforma, together with the sophistication and elegance of the shops, give this town of 30,000 a large-city air. But it is the twisting and narrow arcaded streets branching off from here that provide its charm. This city center and the long curve around the bay have a pleasing architectural unity about them, which can't be said of all Lugano, for the area was involved in power politics from many sides in past centuries, and city planning has thus been haphazard at best. The dukes of Milan and Savoy, not to mention the Hapsburgs and the Swiss confederates, fought over the region for ages, since not far north of Lugano is the strategic St. Gotthard Pass; in fact, it was only in 1803 that the canton of Ticino joined the Swiss Confederation. Yet, characteristically Swiss was the recent decision of the city council to veto the future construction of buildings higher than seven stories. Supposedly, an eighteen-story building caused quite a furore a few years back.

Besides lingering in the shops of the old town, a major pastime is strolling (in appropriate dress) the two miles from Paradiso to Castagnola, as the opposite ends of the city are called. I started at Paradiso, passing hotels whose "wing-collared" names are such strong reminders of a past epoch of tourism: Bellevue au Lac, Victoria, Splendide Royal, Bellavista, Eden, Beaurivage. And though they no longer cater solely to the leisured rich, they stubbornly cling to their old-world style.

One needn't take the two-mile trek at a gallop. Off to the left at the Piazza Rezzonico is the splendid Franciscan church of Santa Maria degli Angioli, worth visiting more than once. On entering, one is confronted with a gigantic fresco of the Crucifixion, which covers the entire front wall and has the larger-than-life quality of most Italian frescoes, like those in the Sistine Chapel. The other walls also bear scenes from the Bible, one of these being the Last Supper with a greedy Judas clutching his thirty pieces of silver. All were painted by Bernardino Luini in the middle of the sixteenth century and are probably the finest specimens of Renaissance art in Lugano.

A few minutes from here is the hub of Lugano, the Piazza Riforma, bordered by cafés and restaurants. Although I am probably helping it into oblivion by recommending it, a much-loved retreat on the piazza was the incongruously named Mary's (why not "Maria's"?), which has the best pizza I have tasted on any of three continents. Rather than sit at a table, since there was always a great crowd ready to pounce on it the moment one made any sign of leaving, I preferred to plant myself at the bar and watch the drama taking place around me. One of the "players" was a parody of the serious Italian at work, a waiter darting around like a firefly, seeming to have a hundred things to do at once—serve wine, scoop pizzas from the huge ovens, toss salads, take orders— all as important, to judge from the expression on his face, as whether Lugano should have high-rise buildings, or open a nudist colony. He sighed, he moaned, he threw up his hands in despair when the waitress asked him for change.

Continuing along the palm-lined promenade from the Piazza Riforma one comes to Lugano's vast Lido, an essential facility now that the waters of Lake Lugano have been declared unfit for swimming. The citizens of Lugano have had the courage to tackle this problem (as they did the prickly question of city planning versus real-estate interests), and it won't be many years before the lake is a limpid blue again. Farther on is Castagnola, with its lovely villas and small pensions. A trolley from the town center stops at the Villa Favorita and, at all costs, a sightseeing itinerary should include a stroll through the villa's graceful gardens and a long glance at a private collection that is regarded as Europe's finest. Rubens, Rembrandt, El Greco, Dürer, Velázquez, Titian, Caravaggio—all are on view and many more, twice a week, to the general public.

As befits a resort town, there is an enormous variety of good food and drink to be had in Lugano. The cellar restaurants in particular have an intimacy due in large part to the very egalitarian way in which customers are seated at large, round, or elongated tables by order of arrival. Carafes of mineral water and baskets of bread are standard equipment, much like salt and pepper on American tables. The not uncommon Swiss restraint toward strangers is less evident in this region, and if one knows a little Italian there are plenty of opportunities for conversation. Perhaps the two-hour lunch breaks customary in Ticino contribute to the relaxed enjoyment of food in the company of friends—an ambiance I always tend to associate with Italy. In fact I often had the impression that half Lugano was sitting in a café (the outdoor ones have the seating capacity of movie theaters) or a restaurant at any one time, eating slowly, discussing, gesticulating. Mundanely, perhaps, my capacity for pizza was never satisfied, though Ticinese and other Italianate dishes, especially fish, are specialties here; and I could hardly walk past a café, reeking as it did of pizza, wine, and salad, without being drawn in to indulge in a by now familiar pleasure.

27. Buttercup-yellow post buses (*preceding page*) carry about fifty-four million travelers and four thousand tons of baggage yearly over some of Switzerland's most rugged countryside.

28–29. Barely an hour and a half from Zürich is the thriving town of St. Gallen (*left*), whose origins reach back to the early seventh century. *Below* is the town's Abbey Library.

30. The curved gables and painted facades of the older houses of Appenzell are characteristic of the entire Appenzell region.

31–34. Rural scenes from the Appenzell area. In the "Alpaufzug" (*below* and *opposite below*), farmers and young shepherds, decked out in traditional finery, lead their livestock up to alpine pastures in the first ascent after winter's snows. Switzerland's rough terrain has always been more suitable for grazing than arable farming, and the income made from dairying and cattle raising amounts to about half of all agricultural income.

◁ 35–37. Part of the canton of Grisons, or Graubünden, in eastern Switzerland is divided into the Upper and Lower Engadine. Characteristic of the latter are the ornamented balconies shown *opposite above* and the architecture of the delightful village of Guarda, whose children have their own festival—the "Chalanda Marz" (*left*).

38. The alpine storage huts *above* are near Davos, in the heart of Grisons. This canton owes its fame largely to its winter resorts, but its valleys also shelter a unique and still active variety of Romance dialects.

40. Two hairy natives of Altdorf who claim to be Tell's descendants.

◁ 39. A heroic statue of Wilhelm Tell and his boy (*opposite*) stands in front of Altdorf's town hall. It was here, according to popular legend, Tell's markmanship was tested.

41. Yodeling (*above*), though associated particularly with Switzerland and the Austrian Tirol, is found in other mountainous parts—in the Americas, but also in China!

42. A girl (*left*) poses in the traditional costume of her region.

43–45. The Benedictine monastery of Einsiedeln, *left*, is one of Europe's major pilgrimage centers. The interior of its baroque abbey (*above*) contains a jeweled statue of the "Black Madonna," darkened through the centuries by the smoke of votive candles.

48. Though its mineral water has been used since the fifteenth century to alleviate respiratory ailments, the Simmental is better known as a cattle-breeding region (*below*).

46–47. *Above* is a farmhouse in central Switzerland; *below*, the welcoming facade of a country inn.

49. Portrait of a farmer.

50–52. The river Reuss splits Luzern in two, and is crossed by seven city bridges, the oldest of which (*left*) is the roofed, wooden Kappell-Brücke (1333). *Below*, becalmed on a Sunday morning and lulled by the bells of the nearby Jesuit church, visitors take the sun at a café terrasse.

53. Basel's "Vogel Gryff" festival, held in January, can be traced back to the Middle Ages, when trade corporations met for annual banquets. The Griffon, the Wild Man, and the Lion, personified *below*, were devices on the corporations' coats of arms.

54. Market day in Basel. Situated on the Rhine, the city has for centuries been a commercial center; but Switzerland's oldest university is also here.

55. An inn sign in Fribourg.

56. Fribourg, *below*, retains the flavor of a prosperous medieval town—"the only medieval town left to us," as Ruskin wrote in the 1850s.

57. Welcome to the "Wild Man" Inn.

58. Like its neighbors Bern and Fribourg, Murten (*below*) was founded in the twelfth century by the Duke of Zähringen. Its castle commands an imposing view.

59. A senior citizen spins out a pipeful of strong tobacco.

60–61. Clock-making was introduced to Geneva from France three hundred years ago. Today, the Swiss watch industry employs some fifty thousand people in over a thousand firms, where the emphasis is on valuable, highly finished goods.

62–63. Geneva, *left* and *below*, has one of the most cosmopolitan histories of all European cities. A Celtic settlement, a Roman city, a Burgundian capital, a republic, a sanctuary for French Protestants and foreign currency—Geneva has always played an international role. The Red Cross was started here in 1864 by a local citizen; the European headquarters of the U.N. is based here; and Geneva is home to an astonishing number of other international organizations.

67. Scenic Château d'Oex, *above*, lies in a traditional cheese-making area.

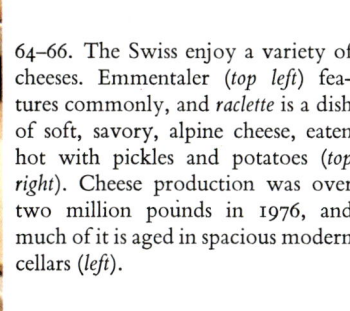

64–66. The Swiss enjoy a variety of cheeses. Emmentaler (*top left*) features commonly, and *raclette* is a dish of soft, savory, alpine cheese, eaten hot with pickles and potatoes (*top right*). Cheese production was over two million pounds in 1976, and much of it is aged in spacious modern cellars (*left*).

68. Vevey, as the center of an important wine-producing region, is the site of a "Fête des Vignerons," held by winemakers every twenty-five years. Most Swiss wines are light and refreshing, and many have what the Swiss call a "star"—a slight sparkle—in them.

69–70. The best Swiss wines come from the southern-exposed slopes of Lake Geneva. *Above* are Queen Bertha's vineyards, and *below* is the Château Aigle, also in the canton of Vaud.

◁ 71. About a mile and a half down Lake Geneva from Montreux is Chillon Castle (*preceding page*). In true tourist fashion, the poet Byron, on visiting this landmark, carved his initials on a pillar in the dungeon.

72. Locarno, a gleaming, sun-bathed resort on Lake Maggiore (*below*), is often compared to Nice, on the French Riviera.

73. Ascona (*left*) shares the water-sports facilities of its neighbor, Locarno.

74. A foreign resident, anxious to try the honesty of the Swiss, is said to have left a bag of jewels tied to the back of his bike, only to be summoned by the local police several days later and advised to treat his valuables—still intact—with a little more respect.

◁ 75. The church of Madonna del Sasso, *opposite*, crowns the village of Morcote, on Lake Lugano.

77. *Overleaf* is the "main street" of ▷ Gandria, a picturesque village only a short steamer ride east of Lugano.

76. One of Bellinzona's three fifteenth-century bastions (*below*) guards the capital of Ticino canton.

Excursions

Whenever I walked into a railway station in Switzerland I had a feeling of exhilaration. It was not one of those dreary structures I knew from southern towns in the U.S., where people who would have preferred to go by car stood about waiting solemnly for overdue train connections. The very air was alive in a Swiss station. There was the last-minute rush of businessmen; relatives off to the countryside; the bustle of porters with goods; and skiers in bright gear. A row of gleaming electric coaches awaited them all. You could go anywhere you wanted (Lausanne 9:03; Luzern 9:10; Winterthur 9:14). The remotest hamlet, the highest peak, were within reach in one day. On I got and off I went. I felt extremely free and mobile traveling this way in Switzerland —and for an American, a product of the internal-combustion society, it was something of a novelty.

Comfortable, quick, and efficient was the ride, and the scenery spectacular. Switzerland is not one long, straight, narrow way from east to west; in between are rock and ice towers, hills and dales, lakes and forests. The road and railway builders have accomplished amazing feats in dealing with these natural barriers, for it is these very barriers that draw many people to Switzerland. Would visitors on two-week holidays bother with the Matterhorn if they had to go to Zermatt by mule (as they did ninety years ago, when the average length of stay of an English tourist was forty-five days)? The railways provide access to the country's natural beauties, and in turn these remote regions have become revitalized by the traffic of tourists and goods that now flows their way. And though that universal custom of leaving the farm and flocking to the city for work does exist in Switzerland, it has been checked to a certain extent by the new viability of remote areas.

Happily, this extension of the rail network to every nook and cranny has not met with financial disaster. The stations themselves reflect the healthy state of affairs. Those in the country are often proud two- and three-story chalets with brightly painted shutters and geraniums growing from every window. Crisp-uniformed men come out to meet each arriving train and take possession of mail and freight—cows in special cages, milk, skis, bicycles. The large stations are marvels of organization and service, tending to passengers in transit. The railroad buffets, little stand-up bars in the corridors of the station, would delight anyone, making one feel like a child set loose in a candy store when choosing coffee: *espresso*, *cappuccino*, *crème*, *au lait*, or *nature* anyone? Rows of spirits fill the shelves—whiskeys and aperitifs, digestifs, wines, and brandies. At the early hour of ten a few men can be seen bolting down a glass or two of wine, and chefs in full dress are preparing the day's offerings of smoked-salmon sandwiches, croque-monsieur, or vol-au-vent. Luxury in the full glory of stand-up service.

Likewise on the train itself: though you can't take a shower, do your shopping, buy a newspaper, or any of a dozen things you can at the larger stations, you can combine nature worship, excellent food and drink, and a comfortable ride. You are no sooner seated and admiring the passing scenery than around comes the mini-bar—a cart full of wine, beer, brandy, mineral water, soft drinks, coffee, tea, sandwiches, cigarettes, candy bars, and chocolates. For anyone brought up on self-service, train travel in Switzerland is sheer hedonism.

For the solitary traveler, one's fellow passengers will always provide an entertaining focus for beady-eyed observation. Still ringing in my ears are the heavily accented words—"Où est la deuxième?"—of a couple from New York in frantic search of a missing twin. Another time three English ladies, well into their seventies, sat across the aisle from me. One was writing postcards, the genteel kind of person one is always apt to see scribbling postcards in restaurants or hotel lobbies in foreign cities. Another, a map of Western Europe held rigidly in front of her, was studying it as though by concentration alone she could etch those alien names onto her mind. On the map was circled Munich, Innsbruck, Zürich, Geneva, and Interlaken. I wondered what on earth they would be doing in all those cities, and idly thought of lines that might be penned on all those picture postcards.

More memorable, though, were two smart gentlemen sitting beside me, discussing their business in great earnest. I thought they must be stockbrokers when suddenly a small box of Swiss chocolates was drawn from an attaché case, and my distinguished companions proceeded to bite, savor, and weigh the merits of each piece, occasionally making notes. Here was the great expertise involved in producing Swiss goods—renowned for their high quality—at work before my very eyes. I don't think I will ever be able to eat chocolate again without thinking of this solemn little step in the grand process of satisfying the world's craving for the sweet.

In places too rugged for the railway to penetrate, the bright yellow postal buses have taken over. Like the trains, these sleek coaches guarantee the delivery of passengers and goods and, with their regular service, in turn contribute to the unlocking of remote areas. The terrain covered on a postal bus, particularly at high altitude, will give an even greater appreciation for Swiss scenery (big windows for alpine views), for the technical feats necessary to build roads in such mountainous conditions, and for the drivers themselves. From Davos to the Lower Engadine, I crossed the barren, forsaken Flüela Pass by bus. We climbed nearly eight thousand feet around never-ending hairpin curves, the driver sounding an electric version of the eerie alpenhorn at every turn and giving a running commentary on the scenery as he drove. When we reached the pass, eight feet of snow still lay on either side of the road. It was June, and we were the first bus over the pass in nine months.

Riding through Switzerland is like reliving Vivaldi's *Four Seasons*. From a climatic point of view temperatures range from the polar conditions at the Jungfraujoch to the subtropical temperatures of Ticino. One morning in June I traveled north from Lugano past Italianate villages surrounded by chestnut forests and palm trees; by noon, after passing through the St. Gotthard Tunnel, I was at Andermatt where the snow on the peaks never melts. Continuing northwest, I went toward Luzern, and the landscape was one of rolling green hills, cows grazing in lush grass, and wildflowers.

Each region displays the effect of the different cultural heritages of its inhabitants. Cool, pastel-colored stucco houses in the pacific setting of French Switzerland gradually give way in German Switzerland to compact wooden houses, carefully planted gardens, and symmetrical woodpiles. The characteristic Ticinese hill villages present a good example of the effects of the interplay of nature and civilization on a landscape. Ticino has a Mediterranean climate, but the terrain is fairly alpine. Everywhere villages can be seen clinging almost desperately to mountainsides, and, from necessity, the houses are densely packed together.

So one is forced to conclude that Switzerland is in fact a mosaic, containing prodigious variety on a small scale.

I rode from Zürich to St. Gallen by train, passing the city of Winterthur, through countryside that reminded me of the settings of pastoral paintings. Not five minutes outside Zürich the transition from city to country begins. First, there are those little city-dweller gardens, or "allotments"—that very unpicturesque, socialistic-sounding English word for them. Lettuce, radishes, tomatoes, peppers, and bluebells are all carefully tended within small confines by people who want to have the feel of earth, not concrete, beneath their feet for a few hours each week. Soon the gardens become farms and pastures. There is something both idyllic and static about this rolling green land, the few farmhouses, and the sheep poised on the hills. The area is not heavily populated, and, as I learned, the number of people actually engaged in agriculture in Switzerland is very small. Thus it was almost startling when a human figure did move across the landscape.

Suddenly, in the midst of this peaceful scene, is the bustling city of St. Gallen. Back in 612, when the Irish missionary Gall came here, it was undoubtedly more tranquil. He founded an abbey that became a center for Occidental science and culture in the Middle Ages, and the exceptionally rich illuminated manuscripts in the Abbey Library testify to great activity in the service of Christendom. In front of the abbey is St. Gallen's most imposing monument, a baroque cathedral dating from 1756 whose vast interior is alive with light and color. The importance of the cathedral is reflected in the way the streets and small lanes have been arranged around the building in concentric circles. But I found the implied spirituality a bit hard to reconcile with the bourgeois character of today's *homo gallus* and the influence of a prosperity that originated with the early growth of the linen and textile industry here. The well-preserved merchant houses on the north side of the cathedral attest to worldly concerns, the joys of real living, among a hard-working people. Some of these buildings have exquisitely sculpted bay windows, and the paintings on the facades are a justifiable record of municipal vanity.

North from St. Gallen one comes within easy reach of the resorts along Lake Constance. It was southward I wanted to go, however, to the Appenzell valley, perhaps attracted by a postcard someone once sent me from this region—of a boy of about seven, dressed in local costume: yellow pants, scarlet vest, a white pleated shirt, and pictures of cows on his buttons and on the sash around his waist. He had a pipe in his mouth. Yes, quaint, but I had half expected to see him when I arrived in Switzerland.

The canton of Appenzell is a sparsely populated alpine region, with homesteads and compact villages scattered in the wide-open land and farms perched on the hills. It has long been an isolated area involved mostly in dairy farming, and this isolation—combined with long, cold, winter nights indoors and lonely evenings on high summer pastures—has been both cause and stimulus to the well-known Appenzeller folkcrafts. Cows have been the main theme, particularly in rural scenes shown on painted plates and in naïve folk paintings: the traditional procession up to the high pastures when the snows have melted, the cows with large bells around their necks; or the sun smiling kindly on cattle fattening themselves in their summer alpine home. The lovingly decorated costume of the boy on my postcard, probably the most famous Swiss dress, is also shown in fine detail on these plates and paintings. Appenzeller houses are distinguished by their curved front gables, and the painted facades and inn signs lend a gay note to the immaculate streets. Regrettably, the town of Appenzell is a trifle on the touristic side, its stores selling much of what passes for "Authentic Swiss" in Los Angeles and Dallas.

Other towns in the area offer more of the same on a smaller scale. Urnäsch, for instance, a "one-street town" if ever there was one, has some good examples of Appenzeller architecture and classic Swiss inn signs. And at the Hotel Krone, you might have their "farmer's lunch": Appenzeller cheese (a good, sharp flavor), dark brown bread and butter, a mug of beer, and strawberries with fresh cream to follow. Everyone is apt to greet you with "Grüezi" or "Grüss Gott," which are customary salutations in this part of the world.

Despite the idyllic setting of the Appenzell region, it is perhaps a little too disciplined. The Lake Luzern area, however, southwest of here, has a more rugged, wild, and mountainous aspect, a "heroic" quality, as if to conjure up the deeds of past inhabitants of cantons that banded together and fought their feudal oppressors. In contrast, Brunnen on Lake Luzern is a rather sleepy, but very pleasant spot—as befits a resort town—and from here you can sail through an area that looms large in early Swiss history, to see the Rütli meadow, where the oath was sworn; the Schiller Stone, dedicated to Friedrich Schiller, the author of *Wilhelm Tell*; and Tellsplatte, the rocky ledge from which the archer jumped to escape the boat that would take him to prison. Readers should be warned, though, that only someone with more than a passing interest in these themes would want to get off the cozy boat at this point and view these places. There is hardly a toehold to be had, as the land here rises sharply from the water's edge, and it is easy to see why the early confederates were often left pretty much alone: their homes were inaccessible, and aggressors, rowing up in boats, not infrequently lost heart when boulders crashed down upon them from the cliffs above. In memory of Tell, since I had often enjoyed the play by Schiller, I made a side trip to Altdorf, where the archer is supposed to have shot the apple from his son's head. In the town hall square was an imposing bronze statue of Tell with his boy, and from there I proceeded to the Tellenbräu Restaurant, hoping to see more traces of the legend and have a glass of wine. But the locals—perhaps struck dumb by the sight of an unaccompanied red-headed female in their preserve—were unforthcoming, and I emerged no more knowledgeable than before.

French-speaking Switzerland has the reputation of being possibly more relaxed than the German part. In traveling from one area to the other, however, the changes are noticeable but not abrupt, for there have been interactions on both sides. I did find the range of countryside in "la Suisse romande" a touch more varied than in east Switzerland, perhaps because the orderliness and industry of the latter impart a certain uniformity to the landscape; but in Montreux, which is situated on Lake Geneva and is one of Europe's most gracious resorts, it is the spectacular combination of nature (the peak of the Dent d'Oche is just across the lake) and the intense cultivation of land (the vineyards) that forms its appeal. The surrounding mountains protect it from harsh weather, and its fine, open location draws great crowds to the outdoor cafés and restaurants. The view and the lightness of the air are tonic. It was sitting in one of those cafés that I watched a group of Swiss schoolchildren below me in the street. There were six or seven of them, and they were sitting, lying, kneeling, running around on the sidewalk, drawing pictures of the mountains. Occasionally a car would drive by, and their unattended papers would scatter in all directions, eliciting great squeals of hilarity.

Among my store of antique postcards is one about fifty years old of a view of Montreux from inside the coach of the Montreux–Bernese Oberland Railway. Two ladies dressed in the chic style of the 1920s sit on plush velvet seats (the floor of the coach is carpeted), and through the picture window they look down on

Montreux, set in its curving bay. A large white steamer plies the blue lake, and the looming mountains across from Montreux complete the scene. This railway goes all the way to Interlaken and Luzern, the "Golden Pass Route" according to my postcard, and I followed the same route—minus the velvet upholstery and carpets. The view in spring was as magnificent as theirs had been. Hardly half an hour from Montreux the Alps begin. Rolling green hills, with cows standing up to their haunches in lush pastures, and daffodils and narcissus growing everywhere. Chalets cling to hills and dot the roads (a St. Bernard actually stood in front of one), and villages cluster in valleys dominated by snow-capped towers—some valleys so peaceful that only the sound of cowbells can be heard.

An hour up a tremendously steep incline and we reached Château d'Oex, an attractive alpine resort just over the mountain from its more famous neighbor, Gstaad. Like Gstaad, it is set deep in an amphitheater of mountains whose slopes draw hosts of skiers every winter, and its many chalets are where most of them put up for their vacations, in winter and summer. Though its facilities for year-round amusement are not quite so extensive as Gstaad's, there is inevitably less of a strain on those facilities. And though Château d'Oex is a little on the conservative side— no high-rises, all houses must be in the chalet style—the intention is reasonable: after all, the tourists only stay a while, the inhabitants have to live here. The general feeling also seems to be that if people want a wild night life they can drive over to Gstaad to participate in it, though there's no dearth of social amenities in Château d'Oex itself. It is a beautiful place, for those who are serious about their sports but are not slavish camp-followers of the more fashionable resorts.

Like Appenzell, the area around Château d'Oex has traditionally been a dairy-farming one, and it was here that I got to see a cheese-making demonstration at a restaurant called Le Chalet. Despite this first-hand experience, I still find the process a rather mysterious one. From what I gathered, though, the following things are necessary when making cheese. The first ingredient in the process is a very solid, competent individual with curly gray hair and bright blue eyes. Next is a wood fire blazing away, and a twenty-four-gallon cauldron over it. According to my estimate this amount of milk will produce about thirteen pounds of cheese, as six quarts are needed for every pound. The milk in the cauldron is heated to approximately 90°F., and a starter of rennet and an acid culture are added that eventually cause the milk to undergo certain changes, of which the most important is coagulation. Our sturdy veteran stirs the mixture constantly to keep the rennet evenly distributed until the magic coagulation takes place, all the while checking his fire to ensure it remains constant. Then, with a metal instrument resembling a harp, the coagulated mixture is cut into small cubes, separating the curd from the whey. By very delicate acrobatics the curd mass is then lifted from the cauldron in a cheese cloth, flopped a bit to extract whey moisture, and then placed in a wheel to be pressed. Pressure expels the excess moisture and helps to form the rind. (What I did not see was the placing of the cheese in a cold cellar, the brine bath, the days in a warm cellar, and the months of ripening.) This is the barest outline of what happened, and after all this the rhyme "Little Miss Muffet sat on a tuffet, eating her curds and whey" remains as puzzling to me as it did the first time I heard it, twenty-five years ago. How can one eat whey (it's a liquid), and who would want to eat curd?

If you visit nearby Gruyères, you can also see the process there, but this is carried out on a much grander scale, with thousand-gallon cauldrons, automatic mixing and harping, and slides and narration in three languages. The cheese-makers there don't get rough red cheeks from wood fires, since the heating is controlled electrically. (A couple of times I ventured close to the fire to watch our man in Château d'Oex at work, but the heat always drove me back to the safety of my table and a glass of wine.)

Again, as in Appenzell, the farmers in the Château d'Oex region have plenty of time on their hands on long winter evenings. But theirs are not idle hands, and the museum in Château d'Oex—which must be the best-preserved regional museum in Switzerland—contains a loving record of their labors and some fine specimens of the folk arts of this region: tools used by local craftsmen (blacksmiths, roofers, harness-makers, weavers, and shoemakers); irons for making waffles and wafer biscuits dating from the sixteenth century; and a coffee mill from 1690. Perhaps the most eye-appealing exhibits are the minutely detailed papercuts by J. J. Hauswirth— a local charcoal burner, woodcutter, and poet—that show cows on their way to alpine pastures and other scenes of Swiss country life.

Appenzell and Château d'Oex thus have much in common, despite their different religious, linguistic, and cultural heritages. But if you want to make unassailable generalizations about differences in life-styles, then travel to Romainmôtier, northwest of Lausanne. It is hard to believe that two such different towns as Appenzell and Romainmôtier (what names these places have!) could owe allegiance to the same flag. The densely built houses of Romainmôtier surround and are completely dominated by St. Pierre Cathedral, the oldest Romanesque cathedral in Switzerland. Time seems to have stood still in this rustic, untroubled place, enclosed by forests rather than the open ranges of Appenzell. The splendid cathedral, now being restored, seems to give purpose to the town, and a number of artists and craftspeople have been drawn here in recent years, to pursue their lives and work in quiet privacy. There is activity afoot, but the manner seems unstrenuous. Next to the cathedral is the old prior's house, a castlelike building purchased a number of years ago by the Swiss writer Katherine von Arx. Part of the priory is set aside as a tearoom whose comfortable old couches, solid wood tables, cupboards and shelves piled with books and magazines reminded me of the interior of an English tea lounge. Take note, this is probably the only "castle" in Switzerland where you can buy homemade pies.

Northward from Lausanne and Montreux is the canton of Fribourg, a bilingual region. The architecture of two of its towns, Murten and Fribourg, reflects their similar histories. Fribourg was founded in 1157 by the Zähringen family that later put its ideas on city planning to work in Bern. Like Bern, Fribourg has arcades and wide cobblestone streets. The houses down by the river are of merchant origin, since Fribourg was a town of weavers and tanners, dyers and blacksmiths; up by the cathedral are the more patrician mansions. A memorable view of this medieval town can be had from the rue de Lorette, way above the town; from here, orange roofs spill down to the River Sarine. On closer inspection, though, Fribourg seems a little somnolent, lacking Bern's dynamism; its station, moreover, in the new part of town, is an undistinguished piece of urban architecture with little grace, and despite the pleasingly medieval aspect of the Old City and its fine historical monuments, the area is a little off the beaten track, a little neglected.

On the funicular from the new part of Fribourg down to the Old City, I met twelve-year-old Charles, who became my guide for the morning. It was a novelty to encounter a youngster so knowledgeable about his own city, and the tour he provided of the thirteenth-century Cathedral of St. Nicolas, the sixteenth-century town hall, the fountains, and the Gothic-fronted houses ranks high on my list of sightseeing experiences. In my halting French

I asked questions and they were seriously answered. I tried to remember myself at the age of twelve, and wondered if I would have handled a "grown-up" with such dignity. We finished off our tour with a look at Fribourg from the Planche Supérieure, where his home was, and I was invited to meet his family. Charles had another rare trait—the ability to judge how well a foreigner understood his language and to speak accordingly—and he insisted that his mother speak French more slowly to me. A total stranger, who could understand about fifty per cent of the conversation and reply to only about half of that, I was welcomed like a family member.

From Fribourg there is a direct train connection to Murten, and I headed that way as dark clouds heralded wet weather. The rain was barely holding off as I arrived, and periodically great blobs of water would slap me in the face. I decided, however, to sacrifice dryness for a look around. I'm glad I did, for Murten is truly one of those places that bring a mind's-eye image suddenly and brightly to life, even in the rain: an imposing castle, pretty houses, cobbled streets, multitowered walls, and geraniums blooming everywhere. The arcades are again similar to those of Bern, and one needs no more than a cursory inspection to recognize this as a Zähringen town. Murten has a city wall, the best-preserved city fortifications in Switzerland, and it was from here, in 1476, that the town fought a bloody, but decisive, battle for the Swiss Confederation against Charles the Bold of Burgundy. Charming places like this are usually tourist traps, but Murten has escaped that fate, and has far more to offer than the sale of picture postcards and souvenirs.

The rain finally became too much for me, and after a short stop at one of the cafés under the arcades I beat a hasty retreat to the station. There I had my second interesting encounter with a Swiss that day, an ancient who quickly waxed fierce when asked about his fellow countrymen. I had occasionally heard a few negative remarks from young Swiss about their country ("Defend Switzerland, all for chocolate?"), but this old fellow from Murten gave me an earful, and his comments—for their rarity alone, perhaps—are worth recording. The Swiss, he felt, were "egoistic, narrow-minded, uninteresting, self-righteous, and wouldn't give you ten centimes if you needed it." The town of Kerzers, where I was then heading, was full of "repulsive people," and he himself was shortly leaving for retirement in France. Eccentric, yes, and a far cry from the impressions I had formed; but his views are an echo of what Denis de Rougemont, the Swiss intellectual, wrote: that for the "great" Swiss there were only three possibilities—to become invisible, make oneself useful, or emigrate (which in turn sounds like Joyce on Irishmen).

When one travels south from Luzern and emerges from the nine-mile St. Gotthard Tunnel, one enters what seems to be a new country. The crisp alpine air of central Switzerland has been left behind, and things one associates with almost year-round sunshine are at hand—palm trees and chestnut forests, mimosa and magnolias, reckless growth and diversity of vegetation. What the human hand touches here differs from its work up north; a different spirit has constructed the villages that seem to grow out of the hills. This is Ticino, culturally very much like bordering Italy, and despite the presence of three international resorts, it is a largely unspoiled, unexplored area. Time might have stopped at about 1800 in some of these remote, quiet enclaves with their modest churches and chapels, their sloping bell towers. Such sites as Scareglia, Taverne, Tesserete, Curtina, Maggia, Sonogno, and Brione have changed little over the intervening centuries, and 500-year-old houses tend to look their age. Sit with the locals over a glass of wine in a *grotto*, a café with tree-shaded granite tables, and watch life go by, slowly.

These secluded places are best explored on foot, by those with time to spare, as are Locarno and Ascona—two resorts situated on Lake Maggiore, with that romantic air shared by all southern lakeside places. Locarno, of course, is a celebrity, whose best hotels cater to the wealthy and elegant, and whose expensive arcade stores specialize in antiques, haute couture, and art. Ascona, just down the lake, has if anything a more "painterly" air to its quiet streets behind the lake road, its pastel-colored houses and serene gardens, its boutiques and art shops, galleries and cafés.

Most visitors spend fairly long vacations here. Travelers on package tours will not appreciate fully the well-tended tennis courts, golf courses, pleasure grounds along the lake, boating, cultural events, and outings to the valleys. These treats are best savored by those with greater leisure. Tourism in Switzerland, after all, evolved in the nineteenth century to suit the demands of people on such leisurely holidays, and an appetite for the time-honored amusements of a Continental holiday will be satisfied in either Locarno or Ascona.

Twenty minutes from Lugano by steamer is Gandria, an attractive village whose houses rise tierlike from the water's edge. One disembarks at Gandria to climb a flight of steps, pass through a doorway, and enter the village—not without the feeling of entering a private and almost deserted domain. Indeed, I couldn't escape the impression that I had wandered onto some stage set, not unlike one of those collapsible towns in Western movies; but as you prowl through the narrow passageways and up the uneven steps (all paths lead on high to the Catholic church), you will spy some signs of life in this traffic-free town: laundry hanging out to dry, begonias in flower boxes, and dark-eyed proprietresses in the doorways of their shops.

All along the shores of Lake Lugano people eat and drink in

little loggias built out over the lake, usually overhung with wisteria, and Gandria has its share of them. I stopped at the doors of several, trying to decide between *pesca del mare* and *lasagna verde*. The best fare always seemed to be seafood with wine, drunk in this part of the world from a *boccalino*, a small pottery jug resembling a cream pitcher. It was in one of these places that I saw a most curious couple, who seemed to combine the outward gravity and the humor with which Italians approach life. They walked in, all 5' 4" of them, accompanied by a monstrous beagle. The husband looked hen-pecked, the wife long-suffering. They didn't have to say a thing, their life story seemed written on their faces: years of resentment—toward each other, their ungrateful children, the greengrocer, the butcher, the priest, the boss. The beagle was the only faithful thing left. Glumly they took their seats and ordered drinks. Soon they were talking with a man from the next table, obviously an old friend. And what had oppressed them five minutes before suddenly disappeared, and they were laughing brightly and loudly with their companion, as if sitting in a lakeside restaurant, enjoying their wine, and talking with their friend was all that mattered in the world.

From Gandria you might continue by steamer down to any of several other villages on the lake. I went to Morcote. From the boat Morcote is strikingly pretty; a row of peaceful color-washed houses with arcades lines the lakeside street, and the tall tower of a church dominates the small town. I think it was a hundred and sixty steps I climbed to the thirteenth-century Madonna del Sasso, an effort rewarded by a look at its richly decorated interior and a view over Morcote's weathered houses. The church's cemetery was as fascinating as any that I saw in Switzerland. Along with a profusion of flowers, most of the graves had pictures of the deceased on them. Often I have walked through cemeteries, and such carved information as "1910–1921" always sets me wondering—why did he die so young, and what kind of person was he? In Morcote, one's imagination is helped by portraits, some smiling, some serious. There are a couple of angelic curly-headed tots, drawn away too early to their heavenly home. And the intense, aristocratic faces and drooping moustaches of the Martinelli family, represented back to father, d. 1886, look like participants in the Mexican Revolution. There is even a legend about the Morcote cemetery: inhabitants of the town who have died and been buried away from their birthplace return, as pale shadows, on the night of November 2, to meet their contemporaries in their rightful resting place, on their native soil. And the legend seems to underline a reality I found, to greater and lesser degree, throughout Switzerland: an attachment to the traditions of home soil, be it a hill village or a valley, a castle town or a plateau.

The Playground of Europe

Switzerland, at the crossroads of Europe, was a travel destination long before the annual pilgrimages of modern travelers. Today, as we eat and drink at practically any altitude, or gape in admiration at the panorama of mountains and glaciers from the Jungfraujoch (after an impressive journey there by an electric railway that crosses the Eiger Glacier and tunnels through two and a half miles of the Eiger Wall itself up to the 11,333-foot viewing station), we should reflect a moment on the trials of some of those early visitors to Switzerland. Think of Hannibal's ordeals as the general drove his thirty-eight elephants over the Alps in 218 B.C. in an effort to storm Rome. Or consider the 260,000 faithful who climbed the mountains to Einsiedeln in 1710 to visit the sacred shrine of the "Black Madonna." And no railways carried the liver-sufferers to St. Moritz to partake of the waters, several hundred years ago.

We feel today that Switzerland has been blessed by nature in ways that few countries can rival. But history doesn't record that these early visitors came for the view or that they crossed the mountains for the exercise. That came later. The English, and a smattering of other foreigners, are credited with initiating Switzerland's "golden age of tourism" in the nineteenth century. On their travels through the Continent, Byron, Ruskin, and other early romantic pioneers, as well as Nietzsche and Mark Twain, stopped in Switzerland to record glowing descriptions of glaciers and peaks.

These authors obviously enjoyed a wider audience than mine, and it wasn't long before literate vacationers were making their way to Switzerland to admire the views. The health-restoring benefits of Switzerland's climate were also quickly recognized, and the Swiss, normally conservative when faced with new trends, responded with foresight and alacrity to the situation. The first steamers were built in 1823. Hotels and health resorts sprang up. Railroads were built. And late nineteenth-century accounts already describe an "invasion" of English tourists: in 1859, St. Moritz reported 450 visitors; by 1910 the figure had jumped to 10,000.

Most of Switzerland's now famous winter resorts began as summer health retreats. The next stage in Switzerland's transformation into a "playground" was the advent of winter sports. The snow- and mountain-poor English really took to the mountains and can claim much of the credit for the propagation of winter sports in Switzerland. Around 1890 they introduced Norwegian skis to the Bernese Oberland, and by 1910 hotels were in the business of catering to enthusiasts of this new pastime. At first, skiing was truly the province of the adventurous few, and in those early days, laden with heavy wooden skis, one trudged up every mile that one skied down. In his book on the Bernese Oberland, Sir Arnold Lunn describes the amazement of one young skier on hearing that Lunn had skied down from the Schilthorn forty years earlier. How had he got to the top (9,748 ft.)? By mule, perhaps? With the opening of the Jungfrau railway in 1912, however, an entire mountain complex was literally waiting to be explored. The complete exploitation of the mountains for skiing purposes and the transformation of skiing into a sport for the masses were finally accomplished with the addition of ski lifts and, later, cable cars.

Not all those nineteenth-century visitors were so athletically inclined, numbers of them being quite content to let themselves be transported by mule or train to higher levels. But many were soon drawn by the upward call, and the English contributed as much to climbing merely for the pleasure of the sport as they did to skiing. (Naturally enough, the Swiss had been trudging about the mountains for centuries and were quite astonished that anyone would climb them who didn't have to.) A fair number of the famous peaks of the Jungfrau region, including the Eiger (but not the North Face, which only twentieth-century skill and courage would overcome), were conquered in the nineteenth century by British amateurs. Leslie Stephen, the father of writer Virginia Woolf, was an ardent admirer of the Alps, made many first ascents (the Jungfraujoch, 11,333 ft., and Schreckhorn, 13,385 ft.), and wrote a book entitled appropriately *The Playground of Europe*. Even lesser features had their devotees. Byron climbed up to the Kleine Scheidegg (6,763 ft.) in 1816. Today, no matter how often a peak has been scaled before, the challenges of rock and ice craft remain. And Switzerland has no dearth of mountains or mountaineering schools.

Very few places in the world can match Switzerland for sports facilities, instruction, superb natural conditions, or the very important social activities that seem to burgeon at high altitudes. Winter holidays here are perhaps more spectacular, but the valleys and sunlit paths of summer afternoons have, in their own way, equivalent pleasures to offer; and for those determined not to stir from a striped deck chair, the Tourist Office's slogan ("Travel in Europe—Rest in Switzerland") will be sufficient encouragement.

There are three areas representative of what these Swiss resorts have to offer: the Bernese Oberland, which comprises the better-known resorts of the Jungfrau region (Grindelwald, Mürren, and Lauterbrunnen) and those on Lakes Thun and Brienz; the canton of Grisons, among whose holiday centers are Arosa, Davos, Klosters, St. Moritz, Pontresina, and the triad of Scuol-Tarasp-Vulpera; and Zermatt in the canton of Valais. Basically, Swiss resorts have two seasons: a winter one lasting from December until April, and a summer one from June until October, though these dates are approximate.

One theory of mountaineering has it that one climbs not to enjoy the view from the top, but to appreciate the mountains directly from below. It was a chair lift that brought me as close to this vantage point as I'm ever likely to get. I had gone with a friend from Interlaken to Grindelwald (3,391 ft.), one of the stops on the journey to the Jungfraujoch, and though I hesitated a moment about paying twenty francs to take the lift from Grindelwald to First (7,218 ft.), I was never to regret a franc spent in this manner. One is swooped up in one's chair, gliding above the chalets and gardens and hikers, the world happily silent except for the rich metallic clanking of cowbells. It was like Poe's tintinnabulations, the bells the only sounds in this new world of peaks and glaciers and cool pure air. In less than half an hour we had ascended nearly four thousand feet and had a view of the Wetterhorn (it is said that only the Matterhorn from Riffelalp is comparable), the Schreckhorn, and other jagged summits in the Oberland. The height and isolation combined to work their strange effect on me and force the realization that here was a natural order more enduring than man's. Chair lifts come and go, generations of mountaineers scale and leave the peaks, but the mountains endure.

Awe-inspiring, too, are the views from the traffic-free village of Mürren, the highest village in the Bernese Oberland (5,414 ft). From Interlaken it is a twenty-five-minute train ride to Lauterbrunnen and then another twenty-eight minutes by funicular, which compares favorably with the nineteenth-century trek by donkey and mule, when visitors took everything they needed with them, and women would write of the difficulty of strapping the tin bath onto the mule's back.

Perched on a sunny plateau, Mürren has a ringside view of the Eiger, Mönch, and Jungfrau. The skiing possibilities of its surrounding mountains were recognized long ago, and the slalom was first demonstrated here in 1910. Nowadays, it has grown into a full-fledged winter-sports resort; less well known, though, are its quieter summer pastimes, its hikes among hills and pastures in the company of cows and wildflowers, or hours spent meandering through the chalet-lined streets or just enjoying a morning coffee on a hotel terrace in warm sunshine.

Mürren is one of the stations on the way to the Schilthorn (often called Piz Gloria, as it was dubbed in the James Bond film *On Her Majesty's Secret Service*), on whose summit—if the Fates are willing—visitors are exposed to one of the most breathtaking views of mountains in Switzerland. Here a little advice about mountain excursions might usefully be inserted. Choose a good day and go before the clouds have begun to gather around the mountaintops, as they often do by midday. I arrived in Mürren in the afternoon, in evil-looking weather, but decided to take the cable car to the Schilthorn anyway. On our way up, a rabid optimist with pointed nose, rebellious hair, and stern brown spectacles kept telling his three companions—obviously doubtful about why they had sunk money in this excursion, since it was getting darker with every foot we ascended—that the weather would clear, that sudden screens of cloud were common in these Alps but swiftly disappeared, and so on. I remember muttering darkly that a nation so manifestly successful in taming nature in other ways should be able to devise some method of scattering clouds from mountaintops. For when we reached the summit it was hard to believe we stood at an altitude of almost ten thousand feet, since we couldn't see one yard beyond the perimeter of the revolving restaurant. We were suddenly angels, afloat on clouds. Occasionally a cloud parted to tease us about what lay beyond, and I prayed that the optimist would be proved correct. As it was, he soon lost faith in his own predictions and left long before I did.

The next morning I was up at 5:45, and vigorously awake. The blue sky soared, not a cloud in sight; and the mystery of the scenery, in the absence of automobiles or other moving things, was tangible in the village. My cheery countenance at the ticket window of the cableway evoked some approving words from the Schilthorn flag-raiser in the form of a German proverb about those rising early having gold in their mouths ("Morgenstund hat Gold im Mund"). The truth is more mundane: I was already planning my high-altitude breakfast. I caught the first cable car to the Schilthorn, along with the employees of the Piz Gloria Restaurant, some Swiss soldiers, and baskets of bread. This time I had my view. Besides the glaciers and peaks of the Bernese Oberland, there were the hills of central Switzerland, Mont Blanc and the Vosges in France, and the Black Forest in Germany. We were remote, in orbit. Apart from a couple of skiers about to set off on one of the longest downhill runs—with a drop of seven thousand feet, from the Schilthorn to Lauterbrunnen—we at our little viewing station and the cable car making its way toward us (now more than ever like a spacecraft delivering a new batch of earthlings to a Skylab) were the only other signs of life. And coffee never tasted better at 9,748 feet.

Not everyone is up to climbing or skiing at these altitudes, but the ride to the Jungfraujoch is also an experience that will bring you close to what some of the snow pioneers loved about the Oberland, and the expense will only be mourned by those immune to the images of a new world. As you stand between the Mönch and the Jungfrau, a sea of peaks, a perpetual heave and swell, rises frozen before you in the miles-long Aletsch Glacier. Behind you is the Concordia Glacier, whose ice is well over two thousand feet thick and on whose surface a city of several hundred thousand would find ample accommodation.

The addition of ski lifts that transport a skier effortlessly to the heights has revolutionized skiing, but in the process some of the pleasures of early skiers and ski mountaineers have been forgotten. The sport has been charted and skiing courses rated for difficulty, yet challenges still exist for those who get off the beaten path. Sir Arnold Lunn describes an expedition from the Jungfraujoch to the town of Meiringen, over the glaciers of the Bernese Oberland; besides memorable views of the mountains, the skier's skill was constantly tested by the great variety of ski surfaces.

Gstaad and Adelboden, also in the Oberland, are naturally well established in the hierarchy of skiing centers, with Gstaad providing some testing courses for even the most experienced *Skiläufer*. And among the dozens of other recreation spots scattered across the Oberland, I should mention Lenk and Kandersteg —comfortable bases within access of some interesting though not severe-grade climbs.

Grisons, besides being Switzerland's largest and only trilingual canton (German, Romansh, and Italian are spoken here), is the home of several world-famous resorts, among them Arosa, Davos, and St. Moritz. In the past few years the number of overnight stays in these three resorts has averaged around 4.5 million annually (I would guess that there hasn't been a single spare room in the "peak" vacation months in the past ten years, and reservations are probably made a year in advance). The number is astonishing, considering that Grisons is about twice the size of Rhode Island, and obviously says something about the attractions of this canton's sixty resorts: people don't spend hard-earned money in uninteresting places.

From Chur, the capital of the canton, I took the gallant red Rhaetian Railway on the one-way stretch to Arosa. We passed through tunnels carved out of mountains, over narrow bridges that rose hundreds of feet above glacial rivers, and along paths with a precipice on one side and flowers growing as high as our windows on the other. The infrequent, sparsely inhabited villages in the remote valleys along the way did not presage much activity up ahead. We seemed to be leaving civilization behind. But then we took one last curve and suddenly Arosa in all its glory lay spread before us—a valley with one hotel or chalet after another, a resort with the mountains in its backyard. Since it was early June, most of the hotels were still closed, "between seasons," but though the crowds were not about, Arosa was not asleep; everyone was in preparation, expectation. How could it be otherwise? The flood would soon be upon them. Six thousand visitors can be accommodated at one time in Arosa (whose resident population hovers at around 4,000). By comparison, Bern, a city of 146,000, has hotels with 2,631 beds.

The views are not those of the Jungfrau region, but Arosa's skiing status seems assured since it has one of the best ski schools in Switzerland, although the slopes here are more for the general skier. Five lifts can be taken right from Arosa, and all the ski courses lead back to the village. This easy approach to sports and recreation is characteristic of the resort.

One hundred years ago Arosa was not much different from the remote villages along the way, and its development into an international resort owes much to its location and climate. At nearly six thousand feet, the town lies in an uninterrupted ring of mountains that provides absolute shelter from harsh winds, though its situation—on a pronounced southern and southeastern slope of a high valley—allows a constant influx of pure, dry air, giving it a certain sparkle and glitter. It is a healthy atmosphere, one of fresh bread in the morning and a glass of good brandy at night.

East of Arosa (although you have to backtrack to Chur to get there) is Davos. With 2.3 million overnight stays last year, it is far and away the most popular resort in Grisons. In summer it is a vast touring and hiking territory, in winter its mountains become Europe's most beautiful skiing terrain. From the upper end of the Parsenn run, about nine thousand feet high, one can ski some four thousand feet down to the town over immense, open snow fields, or even to the neighboring resort of Klosters. And instruction at one of the Davos ski schools should make a fair skier out of anyone.

Unless you get well above Davos, it is hard to grasp the skiing potential of the place, for the forests that surround Davos conceal the higher slopes. So I decided to walk to Schatzalp (about five thousand feet up), which provides an unimpeded view of the sunbathed playground that attracts skiers here from all over the world. Some of the high Grisons peaks—the Hoch Ducan, Piz Linard, Piz Vadret—are also visible from here. As I embarked on the path two people joined me from another direction, a one-legged man on crutches and his two-legged companion. We hadn't gone fifty yards when from another side trail appeared a blind man, walking stick in hand, poking at the path in front of him. I was encouraged; I'm a fairly strong walker, so I proceeded up the path at a good pace, the one-legged man keeping up with me the whole way, despite a trail full of switchbacks and deep drops on either side. But I shuddered to think of the blind man's progress, since the very firs seemed to descend the steep slopes in panic, and he soon fell behind us other sturdy souls. Yet, after I had stood at the top for about half an hour, who should arrive but our blind friend, perspiring a little, but none the worse for the exercise.

In the early days of skiing, when the sport remained largely the domain of a privileged minority with time and money on its hands, an aura of prestige surrounded skiers—an aura that massive popularity has done much to erode. But St. Moritz seems to face no danger of losing the glamor with which its name is synonymous. In 1884, the world's first toboggan run was constructed here. Since then, continuous development of superb facilities—helped by two winter Olympics—has only enlarged its prestige. Whether it's ice-skating, skeleton-racing (the Cresta Run), or horse-riding on the frozen lake, it can be done, and done in style, at this resort; and, like Davos and Gstaad, St. Moritz offers good skiing terrain for those willing to pit their skills against difficult problems.

An excursion one might make from St. Moritz for a day is to the village of Soglio (this expedition led to my greatest athletic adventure in Switzerland). St. Moritz, in the Upper Engadine, is in Romansh territory. Life in the remote villages south of there falls under the neighboring Italian influence, and I decided to explore the area before going to the canton of Ticino. From St. Moritz I traveled by postal bus to Promontogno (the bus then continues to Lugano), where I changed to a local bus bound for Soglio.

The most impressive thing about Soglio is the idea that anyone ever dreamed of founding a human settlement there. Our local bus crept up an impossibly steep, winding mountain road, and all that I dared catch on this eye-straining ride was a glimpse of the wildflowers on the hills, like a dash of color from an impressionist's pallette. The village, a tiny hamlet of narrow, serpentine streets and houses made of wood and thin slabs of stone, belongs emphatically in the "picturesque" category. Surprisingly enough, though, the village had some prominence several centuries ago, attested to by the existence of three "historical monuments." If my memory serves me correctly, Soglio was a retreat of sorts for Italian nobles. One of Soglio's monuments was built in 1701 and was called the Casa Battista. (Nowadays known as the Pensione Willy, its dark high ceilings, faded elegance, and polite, discreet management make it an interesting spot to spend a night.) The German-Italian mixture in the village is evident from names like Rudi Giacometti on the mailboxes, and similar hybrids are to be found in the cemetery. Obviously about six families rule over Soglio, to judge from the number of gravestones with Torriani, Giovanoli, Coretti, and Salis carved on them. There was even one Irma Giovanoli-Giovanoli. And I couldn't help wondering how it was that Emily Stocking Dyball, d. 28. VIII. 1891, had found her final resting place here.

In Soglio I found a very prominent marker: "Promontogno, 45 minutes," and a giant red arrow pointing in that direction. At this stage of my Swiss journey I had become quite enthusiastic about walking, and without hesitation I set off on the path. The first ten minutes or so were pleasant enough, with wildflowers, high grass, and the sight of farmers working in the steep pastures. That ended abruptly enough, and I found myself picking my way through a dense, steep forest. It was all too apparent that this was one of those paths meant for true hikers—those with walking sticks and caterpillar shoes and other requisite gear. There were faded red arrows marking the trail, but panic rose in me as I got only farther and farther into the forest, stumbling over rocks and around the huge roots of trees, with no Promontogno in sight. Where was the sun, so bright just a few minutes before? The ground was cool beneath my sandaled feet. Should I try to return? I looked up. The mountain rose practically sheer. What would happen to me? No one knew I was here. Had this been Emily Stocking Dyball's end? After what seemed hours (it was getting darker) and more pep talks to myself—"Be calm, Elizabeth!"—I met an obstacle. No more red arrows, just a ten-foot-wide rock barrier before me, and on the other side more forest. I thought, "This is it; I'm going to have to get my weary body back up that mountain to Soglio and pray to heaven I don't miss any red arrows on the way." Who should then appear on the other side of the band of rock but a fairy godmother, a wanderer straight from the pages of a hiking magazine, with sturdy boots, stick, green alpine hat, plaid shirt, and thick breeches. And she reassured me that the worst part was behind me—as long as I kept an eye out for poisonous snakes! The sight of her had seemed salvation, but for the rest of the way down I was certain my fate was not to die of exposure and starvation in this forest—as I had previously feared—but of a serpent's bite.

Finally I arrived in Promontogno, never happier to have solid paving beneath my feet. Stopping for a well-earned drink at the Pensione Sciore, and feeling quite invincible after my hair-raising experience, I was quite up to the "uno veinte" that the waitress demanded of me. I brought my heartbeat back to its normal level with some more glasses of wine, drunk in the company of two of the town elders, for whose benefit I even managed to produce some Italian, dredged up from the memory of a few months spent in Rome many years before and from high-school Latin. And when I took the bus back to St. Moritz I was reluctant to leave this secluded place, so cut off from the outside world, so difficult to reach on sandaled feet.

Despite the fame of the larger Grisons resorts, there are places where one can have one's sport and still "get away from it all": anonymous villages, little-known places with quite respectable skiing and other sports facilities, which the Swiss themselves are likely to frequent, the slopes untouched by the international skier. Among them are several in the Lower Engadine. Life in the resorts here stands in great contrast to the hustle and bustle of the famous ones. Time spent in one is like enjoying a natural tonic. The air is gentle in the Lower Engadine, not that strong stuff of Davos; and the atmosphere is so pure that the white of the houses and the green of the summer valleys is almost blinding. (The name "Engadine" comes from Romansh, the language spoken here [also in St. Moritz], and means "narrow valley of the Inn," the major river in the Engadine. Romansh itself seems like the landscape—old, esoteric, and fantastical.)

Right after descending the Flüela Pass is the village of Susch, at the head of a string of fancifully named hamlets—Lavin, Guarda, Ardez, Ftan—along the Inn, reaching up to the spa complex of Scuol-Tarasp-Vulpera. This trio of villages has always had its admirers in summer, luring invalids since 1865 to partake of its curative mineral springs. (Besides liver, kidney, and intestine sufferers, those with overworked arteries have benefited here.) In recent years, with the addition of ski lifts, it has also developed into something of a winter resort, though 35,000 visitors last year hardly puts it in the big leagues. Stay at one of the old-world hotels, enjoy the air and waters, walk through pine forests to alpine lakes and roaring waterfalls. It is a charming alpine nook, where the mountains are not crying out to be climbed.

A good excursion from Scuol, about one and a half hours on foot (although the postal bus also goes there), is the trip to Tarasp Castle, a slightly melodramatic example of a medieval castle. Perched on a cliff, it is pure white, and its eleventh-century silhouette dominates the quiet valley below. All its chambers have been restored in turn-of-the-century medieval style, but it still contains some fine collections of furniture and Grisons objects.

The station building in Scuol was the most immaculate I found anywhere in Switzerland. The waiting room was carpeted, and the wooden floors and walls of the rest of the building glowed like all the houses in the Engadine. From here I embarked on a trip by the Rhaetian Railway to other villages along the Inn. Houses in the Engadine are distinctive, especially in the Lower Engadine, and the villages of Guarda and Ardez contain some outstanding examples. Many are whitewashed and decorated with coats of arms and other designs; some are painted in pastel colors and have elegant wrought-iron balconies. In the style of decoration called *sgraffiti*, the entire front of a house might be covered with frescoes. And in Ardez is one particularly fine specimen, showing Adam and Eve in the garden of Eden.

I arrived in Ardez just at five in the evening, and the church bells were in full clamorous voice—much like I imagined St. Peter's in Rome to be on Easter Sunday, though Ardez is a village of only about five hundred souls. What was more, cows—returning from the high pastures—were streaming through the narrow streets to their respective homes. Whichever alley I ducked into, one of these snorting, glaring beasts seemed to be after me, maddened by my red hair and orange jacket!

Of all the things I looked forward to in Switzerland, the prospect of seeing the Matterhorn (14,692 ft.) was the most exciting, and on the train from Brig to Zermatt it suddenly struck me that a lifetime of fantasy was finally going to meet the real thing. For once, reality and expectation matched. To quote a small card tacked to a painting of the mountain at the Alpine Museum in Zermatt: "It has a marked individuality, what we call *character* among men. Viewed from afar, unlike many other mountain forms about which we hesitate before naming them, there is no hesitation here. 'Matterhorn' at once escapes the lips." No matter how often I admired the Jungfrau, for instance, when I saw it from a new angle it was a new mountain to me; but there is no chance of mistaking the giant pyramid of ice and rock that presents its sharply chiseled side to Zermatt. The Matterhorn is undoubtedly the greatest symbol and attraction of Zermatt. It was from this village that the Englishman Edward Whymper and his party, on the thirteenth of July, 1865, set out on their conquest of that "desperate peak." And it was this expedition that gave the Matterhorn its awesome reputation, for though the party reached the top, four fell to their deaths on the descent.

As Davos is to skiing, so Zermatt is to mountaineering. Mountaineers whose names are renowned from the Himalayas to the Andes became proficient on the mountains of this region: the Breithorn (which at 13,685 feet is regarded as the easiest 4000-meter peak in the Alps), Monte Rosa (15,203 ft.), Liskamm (14,888 ft.), Weisshorn (14,780 ft.), and Dom (14,911 ft). And from no other vantage point can one experience the power and magnificence of the mountains themselves so directly as when one sees this range from the Gornergrat, above Zermatt. It is a totally different mountain view from that at the Jungfraujoch. On all sides are tremendous glaciers, then the majestic chain of Monte Rosa, Liskamm, Castor, Pollux, Breithorn, all drawing the eye to the towering, solitary Matterhorn.

Zermatt itself is an active town. Since skiing is in season all the year round here, the streets are thronged with sportsmen, glamorously tanned, clomping around in the latest ski fashions. There is nothing subtle about the colors of modern ski wear; the skiers always reminded me a bit of Martians. In summer their numbers are augmented by hikers who are just as colorfully, if not quite so garishly, outfitted. Zermatt is not a conglomerate of high-rise hotels; most are small, and there are numerous chalets for the long-term visitor. Everything is within walking distance, including the lifts. There is no motor-vehicle traffic, just electric carts and horse-drawn carriages (also to be found in Interlaken), which seem to have caught the fancy of many tourists. Indeed, Zermatt is a good example of the kind of compromise the Swiss have often come up with to control the overexploitation that frequently accompanies tourism. The banning of automobiles from the streets of Zermatt has had the same effect as in Mürren—the village, the people, and nature exist in a harmony that is unattainable when cars are racing by.

Although the view of the Matterhorn and other peaks is better from the Gornergrat, one can get to within spitting distance of the mountain from Trockener Steg, where Zermatt's summer skiing takes place. I rode up there by cable car on a fine day, along with the Martians and their "clomp clomp clomp." A fair number of people were skiing, others sunbathing from the terrace of the restaurant at Trockener Steg, while another group, trying to get a picture of the Matterhorn, was being sorely frustrated by one tenacious cloud. As I watched from on high, the skiers below me were now like figures on music boxes, gliding, sweeping down the slopes, then being swooped back to the top again on the continuously moving lift. The efficient lift system at Zermatt, as in all the other resorts, makes it possible for armchair admirers of mountains like me to get close to the action and enjoy the air at high altitudes.

Down in the lowlands it was still sunny, so I took the cable car only part of the way down. From Furi, a cluster of weather-beaten chalets, I walked down to Zermatt. How can I describe what happened to me at this point? I was doing something I had done numerous times in Switzerland, walking along a narrow footpath, sometimes passing wooden chalets or alpine storage buildings or crossing an old bridge above a clear and narrow stream. Green rolling pastures and mountains were all touched by the pale sun in a blue sky. This was a Vita Parcours trail, and occasionally I would obey the instructions on the signs—"Touch toes ten times and walk briskly to next stage." Suddenly I wished I had a pair of those stout walking shoes so prominently displayed in the shop windows in Zermatt. How I envied the hikers in their plaid shirts, knee socks, and other walking paraphernalia. My urban imagination had been transformed. I had caught the hiking fever. As a wise man in Zermatt had said, hiking is a sport that allows people time to think, that develops the mind and character, beside getting the "engine" working; and I came to agree with this opinion. For me, the alpine experience began with these walks on footpaths; for others it may be testing one's will on mountain rock or powder snow. For all, the memory of these natural wonders will linger on.

◁78. The Matterhorn (*preceding page*).

79. As a year-round mountaineering and snow-sports center, Zermatt—at the foot of the Matterhorn—is hard to beat.

80. Horse-drawn carriages and electric carts are Zermatt's only form of transport.

81. Prominent Zermatt residents, *left*, after a heavy lunch.

◁ 82. The view across the Bernese Alps from the summit of the Schilthorn (*opposite*).

83. A well-anchored cable car, *right*, makes several stops (one in Mürren) on its way to the top of the Schilthorn.

84. Three lucky kids at Klosters, with some challenging runs close at hand —among them, the long Weissfluhjoch.

85–87. Interlaken (*opposite* and *below*) is one of Switzerland's oldest and most frequented tourist spots, and serves as a passageway to the Bernese Oberland arena. Railways lead from here to mountain resorts such as Grindelwald, Lauterbrunnen, and Mürren, but Interlaken itself has much to offer: grand hotels, a casino, and a dramatic southern prospect of the Jungfrau.

88. Clouds, blown like spun sugar, pass high in the Oberland (*above*).

89. Settled on a wide high-altitude terrace, Mürren (*right*) commands a front-stage view of a chain of peaks, including the notorious Eiger—on the left of the scene—and the Jungfrau.

90. Navigating a racing luge (*left*) is "dead" easy: to veer right, drop your right foot; to swing left, drag your left foot. "That's all there is to steering," wrote Hemingway of the sport. "But there is a great deal more to keeping your nerve," he added.

91. Hikers, *below*, pass in sight of the Eiger.

92. Competent skiers, *above*, explore the joys of virgin powder snow.

93. At all costs, beware of colliding with one of these contraptions.

94–95. Contrary to appearances, this St. Bernard is not beating a path to the stranded VW *below*. In fact, these dogs are seldom used, even in avalanche rescue work; German shepherds are preferred.

96. Fate strikes an unlucky skier! But she's in good hands.

97. Stitched on the slope beyond these chair lifts, the faint tracks of expert skiers lead down to the village of Arosa.

98. Victims of the Snow Wars in Davos.

99. Prospects for a future ▷ Olympic team (*overleaf*).

Tips for Travelers

If one wants to make a freewheeling tour of Switzerland, seeing as much of the country as possible and following one's own inclinations and schedule, a Swiss Holiday Card (plus a copy of the Official Timetable) is the best investment one can make. This pass allows unlimited travel for a specified period of time (eight days, fifteen days, or a month) and is valid on most trains, steamers, and buses. One also gets a reduction on lifts, cable cars, and "special" railways (e.g., the Jungfrau railway). This pass must be bought outside Switzerland, through a travel agent or a branch of the Swiss National Tourist Office. The resorts offer reduced-price passes for lift facilities and are recommended for skiers.

The only thing that may be inhibiting to the above mode of travel is what is called "the season." Exact dates vary, but there is a winter and a summer season in Switzerland, and cities as well as resorts are affected. Hotel reservations are absolutely necessary for the peak months of December–March and June–August.

A proper sports holiday will of course be spent in a mountain resort. Some places are more comprehensive than others, but skiing, mountaineering, and hiking (depending on the season) are Switzerland's time-tested and proven specialties, and you can be assured of competent instruction and facilities. Some resorts offer special hobby holidays—tennis, golf, hiking, even anti-stress weeks for managers—where the price of the hotel room is included in the package.

For those spending several weeks in Switzerland in a resort, chalet rental with friends will bring costs down considerably, especially during the winter season. Local tourist offices maintain files of chalets for rent in their resorts. Going home to one's own hearth after a day on the ski slopes is immeasurably more pleasant (and private—Swiss hotel managers are inclined to be touchy about guests in the rooms) than a hotel. All over Switzerland, though, hotels provide clean, satisfactory shelter in the medium-price category. My experience in the resorts was that for the same price I received highly civilized comfort (and sometimes extras like indoor heated swimming pools).

When arriving in a town by train, you can leave your luggage in a locker at the station (usually one franc), or at the baggage counter (one franc per bag), and consult the Information Desk (some are larger than others, but *every* railway station in Switzerland has one) about a hotel. The Information Desk has a list of all hotels in the town and their prices. After you have checked in, the hotel will send someone to the station to pick up your luggage.

Taxis are not the best mode of transportation in Switzerland for the budget-minded. If you are traveling within a city by bus or streetcar (say, from the station to a youth hostel, which is invariably located away from the city center—except in Bern), buy your ticket from the automatic vending machine located at the bus stop. You don't have to be multilingual (but you must have the exact change) to figure out your fare. There is a map of the city on the ticket machine, and the different price zones have different colors. This kind of travel is on the honor system, and officials are known to come around occasionally and levy twenty-franc fines on offenders.

Things to buy: you cannot go wrong with a Swiss watch. The sheer variety and price range are truly amazing. But my favorite gift choice was a Swiss knife. Here again, one will be surprised at the variety. They range from little thin ones with cutting blade and nail file to bulky monsters with corkscrew, fork, cutting blade, bottle opener, and other attachments that only a mountaineer or a fisherman would appreciate.

The monetary unit in Switzerland is the Swiss franc (divided into a hundred rappen or a hundred centimes, depending on which part of Switzerland you are in).

How to get to Switzerland: Swissair is the logical extension of the country's own faultless and efficient domestic transport network. It is only an hour on Swissair from Zürich to most major European cities, stops which will be included in the normal U.S.–Zürich fare, if one is making other stops in Europe. Like Switzerland's railway stations, the international airports are efficient and ultramodern. I have never experienced such painless arrival and departure as at Zürich's Kloten Airport. In 1980, passengers will be able to arrive in Zürich and make immediate train connections right from Kloten Airport to any city in Switzerland.

The first place to turn to for advice when planning a trip to Switzerland is the Swiss National Tourist Office. The main office is in Zürich. Once in Switzerland, most towns have conveniently located tourist information offices, all equipped to give detailed information on the region.

THIS BEAUTIFUL WORLD

The Himalayas
Palaces of Kyoto
Peking
Gods of Kumano
Moscow
Michelangelo
Afghanistan
Hawaii
Seoul
Goya
The Alps
The Acropolis
Vienna
African Animals
Thailand
Yosemite
San Francisco
Bali
Spain
Mexico
Imperial Villas of Kyoto
Journey through Africa
The Grand Canyon
California
Mongolia
Lapland
The Greek Islands
Hong Kong
Angkor Wat
The Road to Holy Mecca
Istanbul
Burma
The Andes
New Guinea
Marketplaces of the World
Traditional Tokyo
Ireland
Australia
India
Cherry Blossoms
Okinawa
New York
London
Sri Lanka
Iran
Yugoslavia
Washington
Rome
Brazil
Alaska
Delhi and Agra
Boston
Malaysia
El Salvador
Venice
St. Louis
Philippines
Cairo
Florida
Kashmir
Kathmandu Valley
Switzerland

In preparation

Tokyo

Singapore